THE EVANGE TOOLKIT

C000111312

7 Practical Ways to Reach Your Community

Published in its first edition as *A Guide To Evangelism*

Edited by
LAURENCE SINGLEHURST

CWR, Waverley Abbey House, Waverley Lane, Farnham, Surrey GU9 8EP

NATIONAL DISTRIBUTORS

AUSTRALIA:
Christian Marketing Pty Ltd., PO Box 154 North Geelong, Victoria 3215
Tel: (052) 786100

CANADA:
Christian Marketing Canada Ltd., PO Box 7000, Niagara on the Lake, Ontario LOS 1JO.
Tel: 416 641 0631

MALAYSIA:
Salvation Book Centre, (M) Sdn. Bhd., 23 Jalan SS2/64, 47300 Petaling Jaya, Selangor

NEW ZEALAND:
CWR (NZ), PO Box 4108, Mount Maunganui 3030.
Tel: (075) 757412
As from 31 October 1993: Christian Marketing Ltd, Private Bag, Havelock North.
Tel: (06) 877 8161

NIGERIA:
FBFM, No. 2 Mbu Close, S/W Ikoyi, Lagos.
Tel: (01) 611160

REPUBLIC OF IRELAND:
Scripture Union Book & Music Centre, 40 Talbot Street, Dublin 1.
Tel & Fax: 363764

SINGAPORE:
Alby Commercial Ent Pte Ltd., 8 Kaki Bukit Road 2, Ruby Warehouse Complex,
No 04-38, Singapore 1441.
Tel: 65 741 0411

SOUTHERN AFRICA:
CWR (Southern Africa), PO Box 43, Kenilworth 7745
Tel: (021) 7612560

Copyright © 1991, 1993 March for Jesus

First edition published 1991 by March for Jesus
This (revised) edition published 1993 by CWR

Designed and typeset by Mannafest Graphics, Harpenden
Printed in Great Britain by Stanley L. Hunt Ltd., Rushden, Northants

ISBN 1-85345-061-8

All rights reserved. No part of this publication may be reproduced, stored in retrieval system, or transmitted, in any form or by any means, electronic, mechanical, photocopying, recording or otherwise without the prior permission in writing of CWR.

All Scripture quotations in this publication are from the Holy Bible: New International Version (NIV). Copyright © 1973, 1978, 1984, International Bible Society.

EDITOR'S ACKNOWLEDGEMENTS

This Evangelism Toolkit is the work of many different people who have modelled these practical approaches to evangelism in their own work over the years. I especially appreciate the willingness of the following people to make this material available:

John Allan	Helen Mahoney	Norman Sinclair
Fran Beckett	Mike Morris	Laurence Singlehurst
John Berry	John Ritter	Graeme Young
Steve Chalke	Sue Ritter	Erica Youngman
Jeff Lucas		

PHOTO ACKNOWLEDGEMENTS

CWR would like to thank the following agencies and photographers for permission to reproduce their work:

Ace Photo Agency/Paul Thompson (front cover); London City Mission/Peter Trainer (pp.25 & 61); Harold King (pp.33 & 55); Christ For All Nations (p.39); Luke Golobitsh (p.47); Operation Mobilisation (p.67)

Contents

7   *Foreword*

9   *Introduction*

Groundwork

12   *A*   What is Evangelism?

14   *B*   Prayer

17   *C*   Setting Goals for Your Evangelism Stream

18   *D*   Making Disciples

Streams

25   *Stream 1*   The Networking Method

33   *Stream 2*   The Samaritan Strategy

39   *Stream 3*   Commitment to Kids

47   *Stream 4*   The Youth Challenge

55   *Stream 5*   The Caleb Approach

61   *Stream 6*   The Door-to-Door Plan

67   *Stream 7*   The Street Dynamic

Practical Tools

76   *A*   Event Check-List

77   *B*   Organising a Guest Meeting

79   *C*   The Samaritan Strategy Study Notes

85   *D*   Community Survey Questionnaire

88   *E*   Just Looking Groups

90   *F*   Additional Resources

92   *Response form*

Foreword

One of our main motivations for calling the first March for Jesus in London in 1987 was to pray for breakthroughs in reaching London for Jesus. Over the years, March for Jesus has shown that there are thousands upon thousands of ordinary men, women and children, both in this country and abroad, who long for an awakening of Biblical Christianity.

Uniting from different backgrounds and traditions, they have broken down the walls of the church – both physical and cultural.

Knowing that the road to revival includes persistent, effective evangelism, reaching people in all walks of life, Roger Forster, Gerald Coates, Lynn Green and I, in our roles as leaders of March for Jesus, had this 'Toolkit' prepared.

It is an outstanding practical resource, with ideas that have worked for people who have made evangelism a way of life. It will encourage and equip you to reach the people around you with the hope and life of the gospel, whoever you are and whoever they are.

Join with us in our vision for prayer and evangelism, to praise God and to share His love with others, that the nations may be filled with His praise and glory.

Graham Kendrick

Introduction

Welcome to *The Evangelism Toolkit*. In this manual we have laid out seven different areas, or 'streams', that your church could be involved in as practical evangelism to reach your community.

These streams are:

1 The Networking Method
Looking at reaching your friends and acquaintances

2 The Samaritan Strategy
Being a good neighbour in your area

3 Commitment to Kids
Communicating the gospel to children

4 The Youth Challenge
Mobilising youth to reach their peers

5 The Caleb Approach
Releasing the potential of retired people

6 The Door-to-Door Plan
A systematic approach to door-to-door work

7 The Street Dynamic
Taking the gospel to the streets

In the Introductory section called Groundwork we look at general principles to help you be effective in your evangelism projects. This includes sowing, reaping, prayer, goal-setting and follow-up.

In the Practical Tools at the back you will find extra notes on co-ordinating events, organising a guest meeting, additional resources, Bible study notes and response forms.

We have tried to take a new look at evangelism. In the past Christians have been well known for confronting people with 'the truth'. However, although the gospel remains the same, for the 90s we

believe success will come with a relationship based –
or relational – model, which means approaching
people with an understanding of who they are and
where they come from. We need to take them one
step at a time towards a personal relationship with
God.

HOW DO YOU USE THE MANUAL?

Each of the seven streams are set out like this:

A Introduction Outlining the general approach

B Ideas File A range of workable strategies

C Action Plan One or two expanded examples for you
to take and use

D Resources Where to find more help

Now to begin. Pray and look at what you already have
on hand. Decide which stream to go for. Choose
someone with the necessary time and skills to head
up your group's project. Encourage this person to
build a core team for brainstorming and support.

We have made these streams as practical and as
easy as possible. You will find there is much you can
do whether your resources are small or great. We
hope and pray that you will begin to see results.

Laurence

Laurence Singlehurst
March for Jesus
Evangelism Committee

Groundwork

A. WHAT IS EVANGELISM?

Evangelism often involves much hard work and very little fruit. What can make evangelism more effective? It helps to have a right understanding of evangelism. EVANGELISM IS NOT ONLY 'LEADING PEOPLE TO THE LORD'. This is ONE PART of evangelism.

What is the problem? We know that the problem God is seeking to solve is that man, through his own selfishness, has turned away from God, and has sought to find answers to life on his own, and in this sense he has rebelled against God's goodness and kindness. EVANGELISM IS THE MEANS BY WHICH THIS PROBLEM IS SOLVED THROUGH THE MESSAGE OF THE GOSPEL.

Evangelism is: meeting people where they are, and through MANY different means changing their understanding about God and Christ. The goal is that they make a commitment to Christ. Most people who make a commitment go through the process illustrated below, some quickly and others slowly. There will be exceptions where people with no relationship with Christians are converted through street ministry, supernatural healings or a crisis, for example. The immediate presence of God should be looked for, prayed for and expected, but most people who make a commitment have had contact with the gospel over some time.

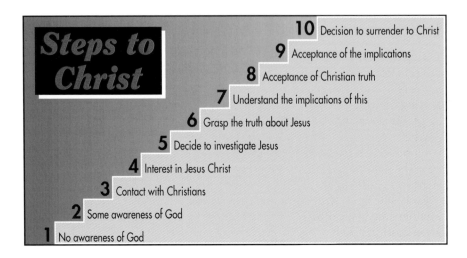

Steps to Christ

10 Decision to surrender to Christ
9 Acceptance of the implications
8 Acceptance of Christian truth
7 Understand the implications of this
6 Grasp the truth about Jesus
5 Decide to investigate Jesus
4 Interest in Jesus Christ
3 Contact with Christians
2 Some awareness of God
1 No awareness of God

SOWING AND REAPING

This process can also be explained by the two words, SOWING and REAPING. Steps one to six are 'sowing' – that is building relationships and meeting people where they are. 'Reaping' is seeing the final decision at step ten. This cannot happen without sowing.

Often evangelistic meetings are held but relationships have not been built. People still do not understand who God is. If they don't know who He is, how can they decide to follow Him?

Don't be discouraged by lack of reaping when there has only been sowing. For example, a church ran a small restaurant in their town for many years but disappointedly closed it because nobody came to know the Lord. But their restaurant was a fantastic success – not as a reaping tool – but as a sowing tool. Literally thousands of people had come into that restaurant and discovered more about Christians and Christianity.

Some projects are primarily sowing tools. For example, caring projects like a mother and toddlers' group may not see reaping. However, they are sowing into people's lives the message that God cares. Build reaping strategies alongside them in order to see more fruit.

What is true of projects is also true for personal evangelism. First sow and build relationships, then you can invite people to hear the gospel in a direct way. They then come into meetings, not at step one, but at step six, seven or eight.

Every sowing strategy needs a reaping strategy. For every desire to reap – whether among older people, children, ethnic groups or gypsies, for example – you must first sow.

PREPARING THE GROUND

For both the farmer and evangelist, reaping a harvest depends on preparation and sowing. To reap a harvest a farmer must follow these three steps:

1 **The farmer breaks up the ground and takes out the stones.**
Sow in prayer – prepare the way for the message.

2 **The farmer sows the seed.**
You must also sow the love of Jesus into your community. Actions can have greater impact than words alone.

3 **The farmer reaps a harvest.**
Creatively reap the harvest by many means – guest meetings, missions, personal contacts, gospel concerts.
When a farmer sows, he expects to reap: there is no doubt in his mind. With a strategy to sow and to reap there will be no doubt of a harvest.

B. PRAYER

To be effective in evangelism, pray! Prayer influences
people's lives.

**Zechariah 8:18-23 makes it very clear that there is a link between prayer
and irresistible evangelism. People who seek God are transformed so that
unbelievers can see the truth of Christ in them.**

In Acts 1 and 2, the dejected disciples prayed and God filled them with His
Spirit, enabling them to reach the diverse cultures in Jerusalem.

The fruit of intercession is seen today in significant world-wide church
growth. Church historians acknowledge that phenomenal church growth in
Korea, Indonesia and North-East India is directly linked to prayer movements
there.

So, to lay a prayer foundation for your evangelism, remember:

☞ Include prayer as an integral part of the preparation of any evangelistic
event, and continue long after its completion.

☞ Constant prayer changes the spiritual climate of an area and makes
people more responsive to Christ.

☞ God's response isn't automatic. Praying may not give the answers you
expect. God looks for three things: a heart after God, humble dependence on
Him, and a life that is holy.

☞ It's the prayer of a righteous person that is effective (James 5:16).

APPROACHES TO PRAYER

PERSONAL PRAYER

Personal prayer is essential. A Christ-centred lifestyle includes a commitment
to intercede for your family and neighbourhood.

PRAYER PARTNERS

Focus prayer on specific situations or individuals that the pair are involved
with. One person can pray at home while the other is involved in evangelism.

STREET PRAYER GROUPS

Particularly effective in changing the spiritual climate of your street. This can be combined with the prayer triplet scheme (see below) or with existing geographically based housegroups.

PRAYER WATCH

For example, divide the day into 15-minute slots between 7.00am and 11.00pm and encourage people to sign up for one of these, forming a continuous prayer chain. This enables older people, the housebound or parents with young children to participate.

PRAYER GATHERINGS

Prayer days, nights (or half nights!) are opportunities to gather in larger groups for prayer – perhaps for people from a number of churches.

Have a programme that allows the Spirit to move and direct. Ingredients could include the Bible, local newspapers, information about the local churches and input reflecting community needs. Worship songs can be effective in the prayer programme.

Two recent concepts beginning to be used more widely are prayer triplets and prayerwalking.

PRAYER TRIPLETS

A prayer triplet is three Christians committed to praying together regularly for three friends each, who are not yet Christians. They also pray for one another and can adopt one nation or people group each so that they don't become introspective.

☛ **How Often?** It is best to meet weekly. Have a clear agreement about how long the triplet will exist. Don't forget that the three of you could start up a new triplet group at the end of the agreed time. By then you will be a triplet expert!

☛ **How Long?** Be practical about how long you will pray together in any one meeting. If you were to spend five minutes worshipping God, five minutes praying for one another, ten minutes for your friends and five minutes praying for another nation, you will have almost used 30 minutes! Above all, keep things simple.

☛ **When?** Find a time that works for you all, when people are alert not sleepy, when everyone can be really committed, and when interruptions are least likely!

☛ **Where?** A place that is reasonably quiet, not too comfortable, well ventilated and convenient.

PRAYERWALKING

Pray as you walk around a planned route, pausing at strategic points to focus on specific people, homes and institutions. It is best to work with others.

☛ **How Often?** Aim to be regular. At least monthly would be important to build a sense of team work and relationship with the community. Weekly would be ideal.

☛ **How Long?** One hour is a good length to stay spiritually alert.

☛ **When?** Choose times convenient to the committed members of the team and appropriate to the neighbourhood. Don't expect to always walk your entire area. Quality rather than quantity is the key!

☛ **Where?** Prayerfully consider the specific area to focus on. Define clear limits and mark these on a map. Collect information from the council, institutions and those in the area. Get to know it as you walk and talk to people – as well as praying. Visit the parts of the area as systematically as possible. Break the area down into small chunks if necessary.

☛ **Approach.** Don't be afraid to explain what you are doing to residents. Place a leaflet through doors or simply explain to enquirers. Do not ignore people you pass on the streets, rather acknowledge and greet them. When appropriate, invite people to share needs for prayer. Do not stop on the streets to make lengthy notes. This can arouse suspicion unnecessarily. You could make notes later.

Stop occasionally, especially at the Lord's prompting. Remember not to pray in a manner that brings unhelpful attention to yourself.

If there are more than three of you, break into smaller groups. Take alternative routes around the area. Meet before and/or after your prayerwalk so that you can share points for prayer that day and pray together. Other people in your church who feel unable to join you could pray at home while you are on the streets.

C. SETTING GOALS FOR YOUR EVANGELISM STREAM

Goal-setting is an important tool for successful planning. However, beware of unrealistic goals. Failure to meet them brings discouragement. This simple process of goal-setting will help you set goals which promote the success of your strategies and build faith, rather than create disappointment.

ASSESSMENT

Can the goal be achieved? Is it possible? Be realistic. For example, before moving house you look at whether you can meet the new mortgage payments.

AGREEMENT

There must be agreement among the leadership. Get all those involved together to discuss and agree on the plans and goals.

ADDITION

It is better to increase the goals later, than have to reduce unrealistic ones. It is essential to reassess goals as time goes on. The situation may change: original ideas may need adjusting, more people may get involved, more opportunities may arise. When changes are made explain these as a positive addition to the original goals. Change is not failure.

AWARENESS

Communication is a major key to success. Without vision the people perish, the Bible tells us. A clear statement of the goal, the purposes which lie behind it and the expected results is important. This helps people get involved. Regular progress reports and encouragement are essential. If each individual or group involved has an independent set of expectations because of poor communication, the goal is likely to be hindered. In addition people may feel left out when they have not understood the goal.

ACHIEVEMENT

Goals are for achieving. On completing a goal give thanks to God and then analyse how and in what ways you were successful. Ask how more could have been done. If regular reassessment has been taking place you should not be disappointed if the final result varies from the original goal.

After all, this was initially a FAITH target. In reality if you achieve 70-80% of your original target, that is a major triumph. Do not become trapped in being over-critical of the small percentage not achieved, while ignoring the major success.

People feel encouraged when goals are successfully reached. They are drawn together, a healthy group spirit is created, strong relationships are built and an appetite for further goal-setting results. This will set the church on pathways to growth.

A NOTE ON FINANCE

Most evangelistic initiatives cost money. You need to plan and budget carefully so that you make good use of the finances available. It would be helpful to give the responsibility for the finances of the project to one person. This limits confusion.

At the back of this manual you will find a check-list for organising events to help your planning.

D. MAKING DISCIPLES

LEADING SOMEONE TO CHRIST

It is easy to feel inadequate about introducing people to Jesus. But the gospel isn't difficult for people to receive. It was made by God for every person. You can be confident and expectant.

Looking at what Jesus did helps. He simply proclaimed the good news of the Kingdom. It was freely available to those who would repent and believe it. Do not fear to make the gospel as attractive and available as Jesus did. It is good news!

God is so willing to make Himself known that you need not worry about taking a person as far as they want to go. So, how can you help lead them to a decision?

❶ WHAT IS THE MESSAGE?

In the parable of the sower we learn that understanding the gospel is a very important part in someone really developing as a Christian. Therefore, it is important that we understand the message we are putting across to people. 2 Corinthians chapter 5:15 states, 'And he died for all, that those who live should no longer live for themselves but for him who died for them and was raised again'. This verse outlines the problem as people living for themselves, i.e. selfishness. God's answer is Christ coming, dying and rising again for us. Our response should be to surrender to His love, to place Christ and His ways at the centre of our lives and in that way we are no longer to live for ourselves.

Can we suggest that you either use this little outline or draw up your own summary of what the gospel is, so that you have a clear and simple explanation in mind when speaking to someone.

❷ RECEIVING THE MESSAGE

As you talk about Jesus, discern if the person has a willingness to receive and embrace the good news.

Don't go just by appearances. Ask the Holy Spirit for discernment. The rich young ruler sounded positive but was not yet ready to follow. Others have a real hunger for the message but are outwardly hostile, like the apostle Paul. This is often because of hurt.

If there is not an inner responsiveness, there's not much point persisting with them just then. However, always look for an opportunity to pray with them. Don't give up on them altogether – they may be more receptive another time. On average, a person only decides to follow Christ after they have heard the message clearly five times.

❸ THE MORAL QUESTION

Many people, like the woman at the well, are unaware that all their arguments are not the real issue, but rather whether they would be prepared to make a moral choice to live as God asks.

So, if you sense someone is receptive – AND they have some understanding of who Jesus is and what He is like, try asking them whether they would be prepared to follow God if He were like Jesus. If they answer "yes", then the Lord Himself is committed to showing them that the message is true – see John 7:16.

You could encourage them to pray along these lines, "God, if You are there and You are like Jesus, I am willing to follow You. Please make Yourself known to me." Some people have an immediate encounter with God. For others it takes a while.

❹ TALKING WITH GOD

If they want to make a commitment, encourage them to talk to God directly and help them to do this. They are entering a real relationship with God with real commitments on both sides. If they do pray vaguely – for example, "O God, I really would like to be a Christian. If you could forgive me and help me that would be wonderful and I would like to follow You" – they may not sense this reality.

It is better for them to say something like, "Lord, I'm sorry I've gone my own way. I wish to stop doing that. Please come into my life and take me Your way." Gently interrupt and explain this if necessary. Speaking directly to God also helps new converts establish clarity in their relationship with Him and their later prayer life.

FOLLOW-UP

Once the decision is made the work really begins, because Jesus has told us to make disciples, not converts. Don't opt out of the responsibility to follow up new converts.

The truth is that you have a vital part to play in nursing and nurturing new Christians. That's why Billy Graham has said that in the work of evangelism, "decision is five per cent, and following up the decision is 95 per cent".

HERE'S HOW TO DO IT.

A is For Availability
This is because follow-up takes time and energy. God is looking for people who will freely offer themselves and their resources to nurture new Christians.

B is for Babies
They cry, fall over, and make unspeakable messes. New Christians are spiritual babies, so don't mutter when your phone rings at midnight with a doubting disciple on the line!

C is for Common Sense
It is best for a person of the same gender to follow-up a new Christian. Alternatively work in pairs, one male and one female. Use your brain and don't give the enemy an opportunity.

D is for Discernment
Pray for a liberal dose of this gift, and be open to the help of the Holy Spirit as you get alongside new Christians.

E is for Example
Babies model their behaviour on the adults who raise them. Therefore, be thoughtful about the way you live.

F is for Friendship
Don't treat the new convert like your pet project – offer friendship and relationship!

G is for Gentle
Don't expect too much too soon – while confrontation is a vital part of helping people to grow, mix it with a liberal dose of encouragement!

H is for Honesty
Be real about your Christian experience – don't fall into the trap of painting an overly rosy picture. The 'heroes' of the Bible are portrayed realistically, 'warts and all'.

I is for Indigestion
Three month old babies don't do well with steak and chips! Be thoughtful about the Bible readings you recommend – a three week study of Leviticus is not a good starting place!

J is, of course, for Jesus
While follow-up will invariably involve the building of strong relationships, remember that you are wanting to help people become followers of Jesus, not you.

K is for Knowledge
Why not recommend some good basic Christian books for new converts, so that their understanding can be developed?

L is for Letter
Alongside a phone call, letter writing is good because the receiver can read it over and over. It's also good because letter writing gives you opportunity to carefully think through the content.

M is for Meetings

Try to help new Christians in the on-going life of the church. Let them know what's happening, when and where, and what will be most useful for them.

N is for Nurture Groups

These are vital! New Christians need foundational teaching. The regular preaching and teaching programme of the church may not meet the needs of new Christians.

O is for Ordinary

Follow-up work is for all of us 'ordinary' people NOT just those in leadership.

P is for Prayer

Spend time praying for new Christians in your church and in your care.

Q is for Questions

Encourage questions, and if you don't know the answer, say so and find out!

R is for Relationships

Make the effort to provide a range of social opportunities so that, for the newcomer, 'those people from the church', soon become 'the family'. Meetings alone won't do this.

S is for Scripture Memorisation

It would be useful if you could memorise some foundational gospel scriptures – and encourage the new Christian to do the same.

T is for Telephone

Make a call, preferably within 24 hours of their decision.

U is for Understanding

Think about what it means to be a brand new Christian in today's world – do you remember how it was for you, sometimes wonderful, sometimes bewildering? Put that 'heart' into your follow-up, you'll be a lot more patient as a result!

V is for Vision

Most people who come from an unchurched background have no real idea about the point and purpose of church. Take time to explain what church is and isn't, and explain the vision of your local church.

W is for Warfare

Let new Christians know they are involved in a battle – but be careful how you put this. Stand with them in prayer and intercession, binding the work of Satan, who comes to try to destroy new found faith.

X is for 'Xtra' Mile

Okay, bad spelling, but you'll have to walk a few 'extra miles' if you are going to be someone who 'makes disciples'. Even Jesus found the discipling process frustrating at times! There will be times when it doesn't go smoothly.

The Kingdom needs YOU! We're back to where we started really, YOU making yourself available to God.

And Last but not Least, Z is for Zeal

Like everything we do for God, we need to approach follow up work with consistency, determination and enthusiasm.

God has entrusted you with a great job – don't allow spiritual 'cot deaths' by standing idle. Make disciples!

Resources

The Hour That Changes The World
Dick Eastman (Bridge Publishing UK)

Operation World
Patrick Johnstone (STL)

Pilgrims
Rob Frost (Kingsway)

Prayer Pacesetting
John Earwicker (Scripture Union)

Prayer Walking
John Houghton and Graham Kendrick (Kingsway)

Praying Together
Mike and Katey Morris (Kingsway)

Pathways in Prayer
Mike and Katey Morris (CWR)

Preparing For Battle
Peter Adams (Kingsway)

Three Times Three Equals Twelve
Brian Mills (Kingsway)

The Networking Method

A. INTRODUCTION

NETWORKING...JUST WHAT IS IT?

Every Christian in Britain today has a network of relationships: family, neighbours, colleagues at work, friends, people met at the squash courts or while waiting outside school to meet the kids.

Reaching the world begins with you reaching your networks. You don't have to start up 'cold' conversations with these people – the foundations of relationship have already been laid. It is important to IDENTIFY, EVALUATE, PRAY FOR and DEVELOP these relationships, living out a Kingdom lifestyle in them.

Jesus used networking to great effect. He invested His life in developing relationships. Unlike the religious leaders of the day, who preferred to stay in the sterile safety of their pulpits and buildings, He was the "friend of tax collectors and 'sinners'" – Luke 7:34. People were drawn to Jesus both by His supernatural ministry, and His warm personality. When His work on earth was over, He left the gospel in the hands of His network!

NETWORKING MEANS EVERYONE IS INVOLVED

It's easy to look at evangelism as being something that only trained specialists get involved in...or to feel that evangelism really only happens when a few enthusiasts make a *sortie* to the High Street to give out tracts.

There is a need for full-time evangelists and street outreach, but networking is something that EVERYONE can begin to share in.

The benefits are clear. It's a proven fact that new Christians are more likely to stick with their faith when they have been reached through friendship. Networking will demand patience, creativity, servanthood, and commitment to the long haul. Networking is about relationships and showing love. People don't want to become your project. Christians are commanded to love their neighbour not just evangelise him! It won't just be about long spiritual discussions – it will mean cleaning someone's car, getting the shopping in for someone who is unwell, for example.

B.Ideas File

INDIVIDUALS

1 **Be Ready to Share at a Practical Level.** A man became a Christian through the 'ministry' of a lawn-mower! His Christian neighbour offered the use of his powered machine to help him out. After about 6 weeks of this the man was so impressed that he started asking questions about the Christian life, and eventually made a commitment to follow Christ.

By sharing your resources you can actually show, and not just tell.

2 **Find Relaxed Ways to Introduce Your Networks to Your Christian Friends.** Invite people round for dinner – a few Christians together with some non-Christian friends. The idea is to relax, be normal. Don't push your faith, don't hide your faith. Invariably church comes into the conversation. Be welcoming, and don't invite the kind of believers who will have a cardiac arrest if one of the unsaved group swears!

Don't turn the evening into a theological fight. One man said, "I like talking to you lot about God, because you don't get upset about it."

3 **Be Thoughtful and Supportive in Times of Stress.** 'Get well soon' cards can be a non-threatening statement of care. Drop into the hospital, take some fruit, offer to water neighbours' plants, keep an eye on the house when they have to be away, offer to be a telephone point of contact for relatives.

4 **Hold a Party for Your Neighbours.** Hold a barbecue – and invite your neighbours. Take the initiative, invite that lady next door in for a coffee and a chat.

5 **Join in with Positive Local Events.** Christians can be really good at asking everybody to be involved in THEIR events while they show little interest in everything else that's going on locally. Good contacts can come from putting a float in the annual carnival though not necessarily with a Bible theme. As a result of this you will find conversations beginning – "Oh yes, I saw your lot in the parade ..."

continued over

Join a political group, find a club that caters for a hobby that you have, get fit at the local health club, get involved in the community associations.

6 **Be a Good Listener.** As a Christian you have Godly wisdom – gently make it available! If people start asking you for advice, don't be an irritating know-all quoting endless scriptures. Pray that God will help you to present His wisdom in a down-to-earth, non-religious way. Expose your faith, don't impose it.

CHURCHES

1 **Events Should Fit People's Needs and Tastes.** Don't expect people to squeeze into events. Give time for discussion in home groups to identify the needs of group members' friends.

2 **Christians Not Christianity.** People need to meet Christians, not just hear about Christianity. A cup of tea and a biscuit is a good idea in a meeting. But not necessarily at the end, when people with children need to rush home, or when those who feel intimidated can quietly leave because they don't want the hassle. Why not stop half way through?

3 **Capitalise on Christmas and Easter.** People who wouldn't normally be seen dead in church are often willing to turn out at Easter or to see their five-year-old do an angel impersonation during the Christmas play. Why not have a sticker or an insert that could be put into Christmas cards, inviting people to a special event?

4 **Provide Prayer Support.** Hold an evening every now and again to pray specifically for people's networks, giving opportunity for small group prayer, news and updates or positive testimony. Provide a prayer chain and follow-up on prayer requests. Most non-Christians are glad to know that you are praying for them when they are in need. Establish a telephone prayer chain so that requests can be called in and follow-up the prayer by checking on progress.

5 **Start a 'Just Looking' Group.** Advertise a non-threatening group that will allow those interested to look at the claims of Jesus Christ.

C. Action Plan!

NETWORKING WITH HOUSEGROUPS A 3-WEEK PLAN

AIMS:

- ☞ To teach the concept of friendship evangelism.
- ☞ To encourage people to identify and evaluate their networks.
- ☞ To pray for the networks and prepare strategy for the future.

1 INTRODUCTION

Spend the first evening teaching on the theme of friendship evangelism. There is a list of helpful books in section D Resources.

Teach, and if possible, practically illustrate the fact that evangelism is lifestyle. Evangelism is NOT:

- ☞ Only to be done by 'experts'.
- ☞ Only to be done as the local church puts on special activities.
- ☞ A matter of sharing the whole gospel story in the first two minutes of meeting your next door neighbour!

2 IDENTIFYING AND EVALUATING YOUR NETWORKS

Identification

Individuals should be encouraged to consider and make a list of their networks. You could use the diagram over the page.

If the person has become a 'ghetto Christian' and their network is filled with believers, they need to pray that God will help them meet non-Christians.

Often church meetings consume so much time. This leads to a threefold problem:

- ☞ You don't know any non-Christians.
- ☞ You wouldn't have anything in common with a non-Christian if you did.
- ☞ You don't have time to develop any common interests or relationships with non-Christians.

Network of Relationships

Family	Friends
1	1
2	2
3	3
4	4
5	5
6	6
7	7
8	8
9	9

Workmates, College/School	Neighbours
1	1
2	2
3	3
4	4
5	5
6	6
7	7
8	8
9	9

The vicious circle continues.
Encourage people to get involved with:

- Athletic groups.
- Political action groups.
- Hobby centred groups.
- Business and professional organisations.
- Recreational and sporting clubs.
- Health clubs.

- Unions.
- Supper clubs, gourmet groups.
- Amateur dramatics.
- Volunteer organisations.
- Playgroups.
- Coffee mornings.

Evaluation

Questions need to be asked about the interests and attitudes of the networks:

- What do they like or dislike?
- What are their interests and hobbies?
- What do you have in common?
- Why do you have the link that you have?
- How can you serve them?
- What could you do that would be reasonable to help them think about Christ?
- What has their response been to previous interaction about the gospel?
- What other Christians, if any, do they know?

- What are their religious views?
- Do they display any interest in spiritual issues?

3 PRAYER AND STRATEGY

Prayer for the network can take place:

- In the housegroup together.
- Using the prayer triplet model – see page 15.
- On-going daily personal intercession.

Highlight that the Bible teaches that the unsaved are lost, dead, those caught in futile thinking and in darkened understanding. Therefore prayer must play a major part in reaching them.

In developing a strategy, look at the suggestions made in the Ideas File or brainstorm for some more.

Use this evening as an opportunity to ask members for suggestions about the kind of events they feel that their non-Christian networks would be interested in

D. Resources

Friendship Evangelism
Arthur McPhee (Kingsway)
Gentle Persuasion
Joseph C Aldrich (Marshall Pickering)
Out Of The Salt Shaker
Rebecca Manley Pippert (IVP)
The Reluctant Evangelist
Paul Miller (Kingsway)
Evangelism As A Lifestyle
Jim Peterson (Nav Press)

Good Question
Steve Chalke (Scripture Union): an excellent evangelistic cassette to loan or give away.

Stream 2 The Samaritan Strategy

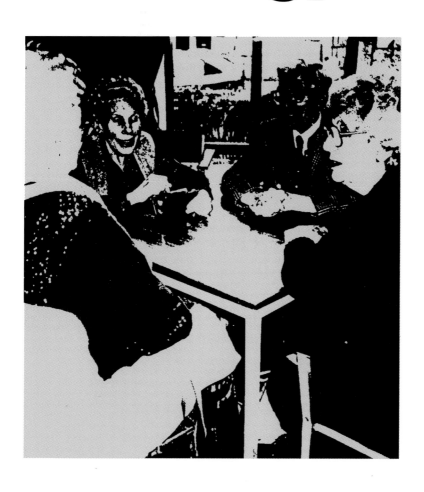

A. INTRODUCTION

Society is becoming increasingly fragmented with much loneliness and stress. Family breakdown and social mobility have led to growing numbers of single parents, young people living on the streets and isolated senior citizens. Things rather than people are becoming more important. Status often determines the value placed on people, not their essential worth as human beings. It is up to the church to show the community that GOD CARES PASSIONATELY ABOUT PEOPLE.

In the midst of all this chaos the Church is realising the importance of BEING GOOD NEWS, as well as telling good news. Individually, and as churches, Christians need to become listeners – with one ear to hear the people around them and the other to hear God's heart of compassion for them.

In identifying people's needs in your community and bringing them to God, you will gain clarity about the way you should respond. Vision will focus, faith will rise, and action can take place.

There will always be more needs than you can meet. Therefore, this stream is geared to help growth in understanding.

The Samaritan Strategy focuses on meeting people at their point of need in a practical way. And it provides a foundation and resource for longer-term caring involvement in your neighbourhood.

The potential for the goodness of God to be released into people's lives is great but BE WARNED – such involvement is costly. More harm than good will come if a group picks up community care as a 'flavour of the week' exercise. People will be disappointed if you don't follow through the strategy. Please, therefore, only get involved in an actual 'Samaritan Strategy' activity if your church leadership feels able to GET IN AND STAY IN.

B. Ideas File

1 **Legal Advice for the Elderly.** This helps the elderly both in the church and in the locality in a practical way. This could either be done on a one-to-one basis by those in the church who have expertise, or through setting up a legal advice centre. The Shaftesbury Society can give advice.

2 **Luncheon Clubs.** Help the elderly in your area. See 'The Caleb Approach' for ideas.

3 **Victim Support Scheme.** This would need commitment, as victims, of whatever type, need long-term consistent care. Contact your local police station for details.

4 **Baby-Sitting to Support Families under Pressure.** Helping with practical needs like baby-sitting can be invaluable. Have a request leaflet or help-line to identify needs and allocate help.

5 **Give Support for Those Suffering with Alcohol or Drug Related Problems.** Provide opportunities for access to support groups and counselling. The Evangelical Alliance can give guide-lines on drug and alcohol abuse.

6 **Support for One Parent Families.** Practical help can be invaluable – child minding, transport, home maintenance, finance and clothing for children.

7 **Bereavement Support Scheme.** Reach out in friendship. Look at possible longer-term emotional and practical needs. Provide access to support groups and counselling.

8 **Support Group for People with AIDS.** Resources are available from organisations like ACET.

9 **Identify the Homeless and Provide Practical Help.** Apart from the practical needs of food, clothing and 'roof' – explore ways of dealing with underlying problems which may have led to homelessness. Assist with contact with the necessary government departments and helpful agencies.

10 **Support Local Youth.** Provide them with a wholesome meeting place. Start a non-alcoholic bar in your town, or give support if there already is one.

C. Action Plan!

A FOUR-STAGE PROGRAMME

The Samaritan Strategy Action Plan uses preparatory Bible studies and a Community Needs Survey. The survey will highlight immediate practical needs your team of helpers could take on. It may also indentify trends and larger needs to help your church get involved in longer-term caring projects. If possible, the whole church should go through the studies on page 79. However, it is essential that the core team of helpers do this. This suggested time schedule takes you through the first year.

1 FIVE MONTHS BEFORE THE SURVEY
A Task for Church Leaders

Identify and call together an all-age team of church volunteers who have previously demonstrated their practical care and concern for others. They may not be part of the church 'core group'.

Discuss their interests, or use a simple questionnaire which asks people to share their interests, practical skills, jobs and experience relevant to caring initiatives.

This information becomes a base for action. Team members will conduct the Community Survey, and be available to assist with practical caring tasks.

If possible, the team should be led by a church leader. Over the weeks of preparation you should identify those who sense a call of God to make a longer-term commitment to some form of caring involvement. Without these you will be in danger of raising community expectations that you cannot fulfil. Explain to the team the time and commitment involved in demonstrating the love of Jesus in action.

2 IN THE FIVE MONTHS LEADING UP TO THE SURVEY
A Task for the Church and Team

The team leader should call seven fortnightly team meetings for prayer, study and planning using the relevant study materials on page 79.

Ideally the whole church, working in small groups, should go through the first six studies. The whole church can then own the vision.

3 THE COMMUNITY SURVEY

A Task for the Team and Willing Extras

The team will carry out a survey throughout one week perhaps following a March for Jesus event. See page 86 for a survey format. Choose the people and streets to visit in accordance with the size of the team and time available. Try to question as wide a CROSS-SECTION of the local community as possible. Don't forget to check out whether there are also needs within the church.

Each evening the team should bring their surveys for collation. Someone should have responsibility for this. They will also need to organise early responses to practical care tasks, eg:

☛ Shopping errands.

☛ Decorating.

☛ Minor repairs.

☛ Hospital/clinic transport.

☛ Baby/granny sitting.

Make sure there's time for the team to pray together and eat together.

4 AFTER THE SURVEY

Practical Action – a Task for the Team and Church

Analyse the surveys to identify trends – such as age, living situation, needs, perception of the community and church, and also particular needs that may require immediate response. Identifying trends helps in thinking about a longer-term response. Many of the needs will be for relationships and support such as regular visiting, relief care/help in the home, money advice, or social contact through communal activities. You are likely to find such needs within the church as well as in the community. They can be met by the team.

They are best tackled by a well-organised, and long-term programme with regular reviews built in. Remember not to start something that you cannot finish or it loses its usefulness because of failure to reassess it.

With situations outside your expertise refer to an appropriate agency. Contact relevant members of the caring professions you know for advice.

The team should make a written and verbal report to the church leadership outlining trends and needs with possible courses of action. Consideration should be given to how more organised, longer-term caring action will fit in with the other activities of the church.

The whole church should discuss the report sharing their thoughts, ideas, fears and hopes. This could be done through home groups. It is VITAL that the church OWNS whatever action is subsequently taken and that the team are given on-going prayer and caring practical support.

Whatever you do it may seem

very small in comparison to the needs. However, be encouraged because as you move forward in caring action, enabled by the Holy Spirit, you will be involved in something of eternal significance!

D. Resources

Aids And Young People
Patrick Dixon (Kingsway)

Building Bridges
Philip Mohabir (Hodder and Stoughton)

Called To Action
Fran Beckett (Fount)

Drugs And Young People
Grahame Knox (Kingsway)

Eye Of The Needle
Roy McCloughry (IVP)

From Generation To Generation
Julia Burton-Jones (Jubilee Centre Publications)

Helping The Depressed
Alistair Ross (Kingsway)

The Occult And Young People
Roger Ellis (Kingsway)

Sex And You
Lance Pierson (Kingsway)

AIDS, CARE, EDUCATION AND TRAINING (ACET),
PO Box 1323, London W5 5TF. 081 840 7879.

SHAFTESBURY SOCIETY,
18-20 Kingston Road, South Wimbledon, London SW19 1JZ. 081 542 5550.

CARE TRUST,
53 Romney Street, Westminster, London SW1P 3RF. 071 233 0455.

Stream 3
Commitment to Kids

A. INTRODUCTION

In 1983 a quarter of church attenders were under 15. Current research shows a dramatic reduction in this. Non-Christians no longer send their children to Sunday School.

T he urgent need is for creative and effective ways to present the gospel to children outside the Church. Reaching children with the gospel, and discipling them, brings a fresh challenge to the Church in the 90s. Jesus dealt with unhelpful attitudes towards children in His disciples – Matthew 19:13-15 – and in spiritual leaders – Matthew 21:15-16. How does your church compare? Are changes necessary to ensure that the children are rightly valued, encouraged and given room to develop in Jesus' Kingdom?

One of the major hindrances that church children face about reaching others is the popular image of the church as 'boring'. Two nine-year-olds asked if they could become part-time Christians because: "We don't much like what happens in church on Sundays but we'd like to be Christians for the rest of the week." A church committed fully to the Kingdom of Jesus should be an exciting and satisfying place for a child. The most significant people in reaching children outside our churches will be boys and girls of their own age.

There are two things that need to be considered in targeting children:

☛ The church must be ready to receive and involve them as Jesus did.

☛ When sharing the good news with children, sensitivity to their past experience is necessary. Some children will know little or nothing about Jesus and will be prejudiced by what parents or friends have said, or by past negative experiences. Family breakdown and other aspects of today's society leave many children hurting. Some will be spiritually oppressed.

HOW CAN THE CHURCH RESPOND?

Give children a home base. Explore how to involve children fully in the congregation's life. This takes more than a quick children's talk in an otherwise adult programme.

Provide recreational times which children can enjoy with others of their own age.

Children are on the frontline spiritually every day in school and need unpressured times in the security and freedom of friendship with others who love Jesus. In such groups the children can grow in God's Word, prayer and the Holy Spirit.

Encourage your children to have faith that God can use them.

B. Ideas File

1 **Housing Estates Programme.** At a time when the children will be around, in a place where you are clearly visible, make a joyful noise! Use fun, music, songs – especially ones with actions and drama to draw the children. Have some of your team visit the nearby homes with leaflets explaining who you are. This helps you meet parents, and deal with any suspicion about your motives. Give the children an invitation to other events in your church programme.

2 **Family Fun Nights.** Choose a time suitable for the maximum number of children to attend. Use active games, thinking games, and team games which involve children and adults together. Encourage 'spare' adults to partner children who are without a parent.

Mix in entertainment slots such as songs, drama, juggling. Simple dance can work well too. Have a break for food and drink. Give a short, sharp visual presentation of the gospel. Make information about other church activities related to families and children available.

3 **Nursery or Playgroups.** For an on-going way of reaching unchurched children, consider providing a nursery or playgroup. In its first year a nursery in a needy area of south east London has introduced 20 unchurched children to a Christian environment. Children love it, parents appreciate it, and visiting professionals are impressed by it. A family has begun to attend the family service and house group because of it! This area of work responds to scripture's injunction to care for widows and the fatherless.

4 **School Assemblies.** At first these can seem very frightening – a hundred or more children, and all your responsibility! But be encouraged – whatever you do in your ten minute presentation is bound to be more interesting than the routine school assembly

continued over

notices! A song, a simple drama and a 'thought provoker' are examples of what can fit. Make your presentation as visual as possible. Involving the children will greatly add to their interest. A ten minute assembly can be the beginning of an on-going relationship with the school. You can give the children a taste of living Christianity, and you will be recognised whenever you meet the children in the future.

5 **Children's Open Airs.** A programme by children will speak to adults as well as children. The programme should contain action songs and dance. The children could write a simple rap. Banners are a good way of catching people's attention. Drama is good too. For conversations with spectators put two children with one adult, and have information about your church, particularly the children's activities, ready to hand out.

6 **Family Services.** These can be a fruitful evangelistic opportunity. The programme should contain a wide variety of short items of general interest around a general theme. All age-groups should be used in the programme. There should be visual impact and audience participation. Clear aims are essential. What do you want people to learn? How do you want them to respond?

7 **Home-Based Events.** A group of children could host this event in one of their homes. Design special invitation cards and name badges. Begin with a non-threatening game to help them relax and begin to trust one another. The idea is to introduce the children to Jesus using a special guest or some other focal point. There should be a time for questions and conversation. The children could have tea together.

8 **Seasonal Events.** Special events like bonfire night and pancake day give the opportunity to introduce children to the friendship and fun there is among children who are Christians. Think of parties at Christmas and New Year. What about a 'Hallelujah' party to replace Hallowe'en? The event could include a short presentation of Jesus. It is important that the event is better than non-Christian alternatives.

9 **Outings.** A special treat for many children! They can be arranged on a small or large scale. Build a group feeling and include some element of surprise.

10 Short-Term Clubs. A weekly club meeting over eight to ten weeks is a good alternative when long-term projects are difficult to maintain. A membership scheme will give the children the sense of belonging. Whatever the style of club have games and activities. Children like both continuity and surprise so do some activities the same each time, as well as new things. Beware of an 'epilogue-type' slot which makes Jesus seem separate from the fun and games. Instead, either mix praying, worshipping and teaching throughout the programme or set aside some evenings of the club to concentrate on these activities. Be sure to keep good discipline.

11 Summer Holiday Weeks. A summer Holiday Week consists of activities for children of all ages. The venue could be a marquee on a local recreation ground or a public building such as a school or village hall. Use a varied programme of events ranging from sports, arts and crafts to Bible worksheets. This is a great way of providing a practical service for your community and making contacts with families who otherwise might not be reached by your church.

A specially designed fact sheet on summer Holiday Weeks is available from March for Jesus. Fill in the response form on page 92.

C. Action Plan!

Fun Event

THEME

Desert Expedition or Camel Train.
This theme can tie in with March for Jesus, having a link with marching.

IDEAS FOR ACTIVITIES

☛ Marching across a desert facing difficulties, heat, etc.

☛ Rescuing people lost in the desert.

☛ Marching to get out of the

desert into the 'Promised Land'.

- Going to dig wells in the desert to provide water and life.

PUBLICITY

- Invitation leaflets.
- Link with school assembly.
- March through housing areas with invitations.
- Children inviting friends.
- On publicity "Bring your sun-hat!"

PLACE

- Near to where children live is important.
- Don't automatically use a church hall but try to use a neutral building.
- Have clear welcoming signs outside the building.

DECORATION

- 'Oasis' refreshment area.
- Palm trees – made from cardboard tubes – available from carpet shops and leaves of green paper.
- Pot plants in 'Oasis'.
- Paper camels along the walls.
- 'Camp fire' for 'cold nights' – to sit around for songs, entertainment.

TEACHING

- Jesus said, "Whoever is thirsty should come to me and drink – streams of living water will flow out from his heart."
John 4:13-14

- Life without Jesus is like a desert without water.
- Jesus does not want us to be 'camels' – storing up resources then gradually emptying.
- Jesus gives the Holy Spirit to be a constant spring.
- Lots of desert/wilderness incidents could be used.
- SANDwiches would be appropriate! – use adventurous fillings!
- Lemonade with mixed fruit juice.
- How about milk 'sheikhs'??!!
- Or ice cream SUNdaes.

GAMES

- Adapt usual party type games.
- Invent games on the theme.
- Different styles of game to cover the range of interest of the children.

LEADERS/HELPERS

- It is important that helpers have a sound character.
- Involvement WITH the children in the activities.

PROGRAMME

- Mix games, entertainment slots, worship songs, teaching, refreshments, quiz.

WORSHIP

☛ Marching songs.

☛ Songs that involve actions.

☛ Songs that are easy to sing without having written words.

D. Resources

Angels With Dirty Faces
Ishmael (Kingsway)

Cassie
Audrey Constant (Scripture Union)

Family Evangelism
John Hatton (Scripture Union)

Hawkeye Hits The Jackpot
Veronica Heley (Scripture Union)

How To Pray For Your Children
Quin Sherrer (Kingsway)

A Letter From Emma
Mollie Thompson (Scripture Union)

Taking Children Seriously: Developing Children's Ministry In Your Church
Richard Hubbard (Harper Collins)

CAMPAIGNERS,
Campaigner House, St Marks Close, Colney Heath, Nr. St Albans, Herts AL4 0NQ. 0727 24065.

CRUSADERS,
2 Romeland Hill, St Albans, Herts AL3 4ET. 0727 55422.

THE GLORIE COMPANY,
PO Box 828, Rustington, Littlehampton, West Sussex BN16 3NS. 0903 783382.

Stream 4 The Youth Challenge

A. INTRODUCTION

Throughout Church history God has continually used young people to build His Kingdom – often the cutting edge of the Church – their energy, idealism and enthusiasm provide a valuable impetus for spreading the gospel.

Churches must recognise this, encouraging Christian young people in their faith, and giving them a variety of challenges to express this faith. However, two factors from wider society hinder this. The well-known generation gap is more specifically a communication gap. The massive youth industry moves fads and fashions so quickly that it can be a mistake to think that teenagers now will respond to the same things as you did even if it is only a few years since you were there yourself. Western education denies young adults full responsibility. Too often their motivation and ability are underestimated. They can then end up underestimating themselves.

To reach young people today, it is important to learn to speak their language. Teenagers are media connoisseurs. Their lives are bombarded with professionally communicated messages. You must use their language to get YOUR message across by contemporary, high quality video, dance, drama, and music – with pace and variety. These methods can explore themes in depth but will mean more preparation than the usual 'preach'!

Young people need discipling. Current church life often seems foreign and boring to them and the battle is lost before you start. Discipleship needs to be tailored to meet their needs. They may need a church they feel at ease with – perhaps mainly meeting with their peers to underline the relevance and reality of the gospel and drawing them to greater commitment. Such groups may discover new, vibrant expressions of church life; making the mission of the whole church more effective.

Young people must be included in the Great Commission. Too often it is implied that teenagers won't be used by God until they are older and so few challenges are given. But a Christian who does not reach out will stagnate. So, involve teenagers in outreach, help them discover their ministry gifts, support them in evangelising their friends, encourage them in caring projects, and challenge them with the great task Christ has set before all His followers.

B. Ideas File

1 **Youth Groups.** Still an important vehicle to meet the needs of young people. They give a sense of belonging, and an outlet for social activities and witness. Many of the following ideas will help youth groups to be both purposeful and effective.

2 **Concerts.** Organise a concert where a Christian group can share their faith through contemporary music. Alternatively keep your eyes open for those that are already happening and take friends along.

3 **Sporting Teams.** Enter local competitions, or just play regularly. This will draw in parents and help with contacts in the area.

4 **Join Clubs in the Area.** Youth, school, Scouts, Guides, sport – they all need Christians.

5 **Community Service.** Investigate what charities and institutions are in your area. Youth group members could get involved in practical help and caring on a regular basis. This should be a long-term commitment.

6 **Schools.** Get involved in a Christian Union, or start one up. Take opportunities to participate in school assemblies. Pray for the students and staff to know God. Organise special events and ask them along. Contact Scripture Union for further information.

7 **Making Friends.** Young people know the local hang-outs of their peers. Go along and befriend them. It is best to go in two's and three's.

8 **'Magazine Shows'.** An action-packed 'magazine show' for youth on a regular basis provides an opportunity for young Christians to meet in an atmosphere they find acceptable and up to date. It can help break down perceptions of the Church and Christianity as boring and irrelevant to young people.

9 **Youth Churches.** To draw in unchurched young people, who may find the usual church meeting inaccessible, the 'youth church' concept is an option. Using a fast-moving format and music, youth churches are introducing a new generation to commitment to Jesus. Experiment with different formats, venues and meeting

continued over

times. Some youth churches use a nightclub venue – including videos, dance music and light shows – and meet at nine in the evening. Others are more rock based, or use the 'magazine show' approach.

While using such formats, the youth church should still be geared to making disciples and drawing young people to a commitment in the wider local church.

10 **Christmas Cracker.** Every year Great Britain imports vast quantities of tea and coffee from the Third World. In fact last year we drank enough cups of tea and coffee to fill 40,000 public swimming pools! But though we pay a high price for our cuppa, it's well known that only a very small percentage of that price benefits the poor who produce the drinks we enjoy.

This Christmas why not get involved with Christmas Cracker's latest project. Has your church youth group run a Crackerteria? A Crackerteria is a Christmas Cracker cafe serving 'fairly traded' tea and coffee. But not only do Cracker pay a fair price to the growers in the first place; on top of that the funds raised through the price your customers pay will also end up back in the tea and coffee-producing countries where our help is so desperately needed.

Christmas Cracker, organised by THE OASIS TRUST and ALPHA MAGAZINE, is designed to give young people from churches all over Great Britain the opportunity of putting their faith into action as they work to meet the needs of the world's poor and demonstrate that being a Christian can make a difference to the way they live.

And don't forget that because your Crackerteria can be open for the whole month of December or for as long or as short a part of that time period as you can manage, your youth group, however small or large, can be a part of the project this year.

For more information contact: Christmas Cracker, Cornerstone House, Ethel Street, Birmingham B2 4BG.

11 **Fired Up.** Jesus said, "'You will be my witnesses in Jerusalem, and in all Judea and Samaria, and to the ends of the earth'" (Acts 1:8).

Far too often our evangelism ends up the other way round. It starts with the 'ends of the earth' and those we do not know, but ignores 'Jerusalem'.

FIRED UP is the youth programme of 'On Fire', a United Kingdom-wide celebration of the Church's birthday, taking place over Pentecost 1994. Developed and supported by a wide range of denominations and mission agencies, its two-week programme of colourful community-based events will take the vital nature of friendship evangelism 'where you live' seriously. It will do this by providing Christian teenagers with the right environment for building strong relationships with their non-Christian peers through a 'social action' programme which subsequently creates the opportunity for evangelism.

In October 1993 a series of large regional training events for young people and their youth leaders will take place around the country. A practical training package designed for use in local churches over the following months will also be available and Fired Up's innovative evangelism project will be launched in towns over the country at Pentecost 1994.

For further information contact Beccy Hunter, at the Fired Up Office, Haddon Hall, 22 Tower Bridge Road, London SE1 4TR.

C. Action Plan!

CONTEMPORARY YOUTH EVENTS

All over the country youth leaders and youth groups are asking themselves 'How can we reach the other young people in our town?'. In the last two years we have seen a number of new approaches which are working very successfully. Outlined below is the 'Nightclub strategy'.

The question that faces us today is not the content of the gospel but the means and the way that content is put across. It is becoming increasingly clear that this needs to be done in a relationship-orientated context. We can see the appropriateness of this as the whole of the Christian message is about relationship.

The second principle that guides the Contemporary Youth Event strategy, is the need to go beyond the dynamic of each event to plan a complete strategy. Often our youth programmes fall apart because we have one good event that isn't linked to anything else. We need a strategy that starts at SOWING, goes through REAPING and ends with KEEPING.

1. FRIENDSHIP

Stage one is to create an environment or event where Christians and non-Christians can meet on an equal basis which is friendship-orientated. The goal is simply to make friends and to be together and there is no proclamation of the gospel. This could be a disco, a rave, a nightclub, etc. This event should preferably be on a regular basis, such as once a month. It should be the focus of the youth work and your young people should be encouraged to own this event as their own, to pray for and support it.

2. UNDERSTANDING

Stage two. Simultaneous with the planning and brainstorming of stage one, stage two is also being arranged. This will be more overtly Christian, but still in its ethos an event where non-Christians feel at home. For example, it might be a series of discussion groups on relevant subjects like drugs, sex, etc., where a Christian view is presented and the non-Christians are given an opportunity to fire back with their comments. The aim is to put across the content of the gospel, but again we are not asking for an actual response.

These meetings would be advertised by a flyer at your neutral event. Again, we recommend that this meeting is done by the Christian youth group with the youth leaders playing a significant role, but everyone has ownership. After four or five meetings it would be suggested that one of them should be evangelistic in a more direct sense. People would be given an opportunity to respond and make a decision for Christ.

3. FOLLOWING

Stage three also needs to be thought through from the very beginning. This is the whole area of discipleship, follow-up and seeing these new converts incorporated into the youth work and life of the church itself. We need to remember that many of these young people will have come from non-Christian backgrounds and will have new values to learn and areas of their lives to sort out. The discipleship, therefore, needs to be positive and personal. Our suggestion would be that this discipleship is done through small groups where relationships are built with the leader and other members of the group. If we are going to go this way, we have to think of training those leaders.

These new converts already have a rôle to fulfil in that they continue to go to our Contemporary Youth Event and its various follow-up parts. In this way they become a vital part of our workforce and the whole group begins to grow and grow.

EXAMPLE

Having thought of the three stages we need to go through, we can begin the exciting task of deciding what we are going to use as the neutral event. We obviously want to work with the existing young people we have and need to ask: Who are their friends? What type of events do they go to? What resources do we have as a youth work in terms of buildings, money and talent? Outlined below are the details of an Anglican youth group that has followed these principles and how they went about it.

The ten members of the youth group and their leader spent a period of weeks getting their own lives in order and asking God for a strategy to reach the other young people in their area. Many of the friends of these young people spent their money and time going to 'raves' in and around the locality. So after much prayer the youth group decided to hold their own rave on a regular basis. Resources called into play included an old church hall (appropriately decorated) and a 'rave' disc jockey who was a Christian and a friend of the youth leader. At the same time they planned the 'Night Bin', a series of radical discussions on various Christian issues to be held at the same venue.

Obviously, in having their 'rave' they had to think of how to handle young people coming in with drugs and alcohol, and all the implications of holding this event. But the first one was a great success attracting 150 young people who were befriended by the youth group and invited to the Night Bin. Over the months many began to give their lives to the Lord and were put in discipleship groups. In the space of a year there has been approximately 9 'raves' and 20 Night Bins. This youth group now has 120 members in discipleship groups and they are beginning to hold more of these events in their area.

This is just one example. Other youth groups have held discos, sporting events or an event centring around social care. The principle, though, is the same.

The Christian Youth Manual
Steve Chalke (Kingsway)

Explaining Your Faith Without Losing Your Friends
Alister McGrath (IVP)

How to Give Away Your Faith
Paul Little (IVP)

The Teenage Survival Kit
Pete Gilbert (Kingsway)

The Teenage Revival Kit
Pete Gilbert (Kingsway)

Scripture Union,
130 City Road, London EC1V 2NJ,
071 250 1966.

Stream 5 The Caleb Approach

The needs of young people prompted Terry and Lois Jones, of Ichthus Christian Fellowship, to take early retirement, sell their home in Luton and move to the inner city. They wanted to give a home to young people in need where they could be loved and nurtured.

Since September 1990 they have been renovating their new home in New Cross for this task, and getting to understand the needs of homeless youth. They have been motivated by the scripture, "Turn my heart towards your statutes and not towards selfish gain" – Psalm 119:36 – feeling that this referred to the pointlessness of financial gain and its resultant materialism. They feel the challenge that their remaining years should be used fully in God's service and to His glory.

In order to help Icthus Christian Fellowship with an alcohol-free pub and youth church in the inner city, one couple took early retirement.

At present the Brown Bear is open Friday evenings for a packed programme of music, drama and speakers – all with a presentation of the gospel. Friendships with young people are growing.

Jeff and Muriel Westlake believe that as retired people they have a lot to offer. Not only can they provide a sense of stability for younger workers in a changing world, but also time, experience, encouragement and support. They can provide a sense of `family' in the area. Their reliance on Jesus for total provision is a good example of the gospel in action.

A. INTRODUCTION

"I'm just as vigorous to go out to battle now as I was then. Now give me this hill country that the Lord promised me" (Joshua 14:11). So Caleb spoke at 85 years of age!

Many of us equate retirement with becoming weak and feeble. This is not true. Today many people are retiring at an earlier age. They are people who are fit, healthy, active, full of experience and who want to serve God. What can they do?

☞ Help reach other people who have retired.

☞ Back up the broad range of existing church activities – involve the retired people in your church.

Apart from more general roles in church leadership and administration they are uniquely equipped to evangelise the growing number of retired people in your community.

To start, build a core group with the specific purpose of reaching out to older people in the community using these ideas and adapting those of other streams. The retired people in your church will have many other suggestions.

Caleb went out and conquered the hill country. He drove out the enemy with the Lord's help and settled in the land, and the Lord blessed him. "Then the land had rest from war" – Joshua 14:15. Retirement is not a synonym for inactivity! With the extra time available it is a great opportunity to enjoy the excitement of serving God in new ventures.

B. Ideas File

1 **Mid-Week Service.** This could be in the church building or someone's house. Use songs and hymns older people would enjoy. This meeting would be particularly suitable for older church members to invite their friends to.

2 **Public Meetings.** Arrange a public meeting and invite an older

continued over

Christian to speak about what they have been doing and what being a Christian has meant to them. Their wisdom and the experiences they will share with their audience will be very valuable. Encourage the church to bring their older friends along.

3 **Multi-Cultural Activities.** Where a number of your community use English as a second language, encourage them to attend language classes as a means of meeting other people in their situation. Start a club where the different cultures could share their memories, interests, recipes, etc.

4 **The Housebound – Young and Old!** Retired people often have extra time to visit the housebound. They can help them stay in touch by taking library books, Christian books and magazines, cassettes and videos as well as provide a live link with the outside world.

5 **Evangelistic Teams.** Offer a faith-sharing team to visit another church for a weekend. If you are urban, how about offering to visit a rural church, or vice-versa?

6 **Helping Young People.** Retired people can be a valuable resource for children and young people. This can be help with holiday clubs, providing a home and refreshments for a group of teenagers to meet for Bible study, or prayer, either for or with the younger generation. You could organise a baby-sitting rota, taking Bible story books to read to the children of the home. Or, put on a Third World games evening or a Taste Life Overseas evening – Indian food, costumes, films, for teenagers.

7 **Holiday Evangelism.** How about forming a team to go on holiday together with evangelism in mind? Caravanning in Britain or on the Continent, going on a SAGA Holiday or helping with a Beach Mission are possible alternatives.

8 **Overseas Missions.** Several Mission agencies advertise for accountants, administrators, medical assistants, and the like for short-term service overseas. Mission agencies would be able to provide further information.

If you are unable to go overseas, then consider the ministry of letter-writing, parcel-sending and prayer. They can often achieve more for the Lord than actually travelling to other countries.

C. Action Plan!

Infiltrating Networks

This Action Plan gives pointers on building friendships with the older generation in the local community in order to reach them for Christ.

1 BUILD A CORE GROUP

Gather some of the retired people in your church to take on this plan. They will brainstorm ideas, research needs and establish strategies.

2 SURVEY THE LOCALITY

What do the retired people in the community do? How do they spend their leisure time? Are there obvious special needs? Identify people that group members already have contact with. Brainstorm how to infiltrate these groups and make friends.

3 REACH OUT TO EXISTING GROUPS

Visit homes for the elderly. Get involved in established clubs for veterans, over 60s, and others. They often need pianists, people to serve cups of tea, cleaners and others. Generous service will provide openings for personal witness.

4 SET UP A CHURCH-BASED CLUB

This could have a mixture of entertainment and spiritual content. Perhaps have a luncheon club, interest sessions with talks, workshops on various subjects, crafts and activities of different kinds.

5 DECIDE A REAPING STRATEGY

Work out ways to present the good news clearly so that retired people can have an opportunity to respond. This could be in the format of a church service or a dinner with a guest speaker, for example.

Christians In Retirement
Michael Botting (Grove Books)

Enjoying Growing Old
J Oswald Sanders (Kingsway)

The Last Lap
John Eddison (Kingsway)

Learning To Grow Old
Paul Tournier (Highland Christian Classics)

New Approaches To Ministry With Older People
Arthur Creber (Grove Books)

Evangelical Missionary Alliance, Whitefield House, 186 Kennington Park Road, London SE11 4BT.
071 735 0421.

Stream 6 The Door-to-Door Plan

A. INTRODUCTION

Door-to-door evangelism produces that heart-sinking feeling. Most people have negative perceptions, and bad experiences. Occasionally there are wonderful stories, but on the whole, people who open their front doors are not that receptive to being told about Jesus.

Is there a new strategy for the 90s? The answer is "yes". Reach out on a friendship basis. Build contacts to help people gain a clearer idea of what the Church and God are like. Find out about people's needs and help them. In this way you build bridges which, if crossed, bring them to Jesus.

Approaching door-to-door work is not often that simple. It is easy to get fearful about how to start conversations, how to bring Jesus into the conversation and how to retreat gracefully if the person isn't impressed. Here are some general pointers:

FIND A TEAM

The first step to implementing this stream is to identify a core group to take it on.

PRAYER

Prayer is necessary before door-to-door work takes place. Pray before the team goes out and have a part of the team stay behind to pray while the others are making visits. Take every opportunity to pray for people, whether simply to bless them or for some specific need.

STRATEGY

It is important to divide the town into manageable chunks and to have a team available for each area. It is ideal if at least one person from the team actually lives in that area.

APPROACH

Be yourself and don't overdress or underdress! Go in pairs, male and female if possible. Though, in multi-cultural areas you need to find out what is best.

Smile, be friendly and don't argue just to win a point. Seek to win the person instead. Use simple language and avoid religious phrases like 'redeemed' and 'Jesus into your heart'. Show genuine interest in others' beliefs and don't be patronising. Try to take a discussion to its logical conclusion. Encourage people to search for God honestly. Explain how Jesus has helped you in your own doubts. Dwell on positive personal testimonies but be honest.

LITERATURE

Literature is usually used in door-to-door work whether it is evangelistic or an invitation to an event. Make sure you have a range of church activity literature to meet the needs of as many ages, races or cultural groups as possible. Tracts can be useful aids to conversation with people who are interested and you can always leave them behind. Be sure to read the tracts before distribution! Consider the various languages used in the locality and make sure you have tracts in each.

B. Ideas File

1 **Church Newspaper.** Print a church newspaper. Include testimonies, stories and photos. Let these stories cover the different cultures and age-groups of the community. Perhaps review a few of the restaurants in your area. Point out some local parks or places of interest. State clearly that this newspaper comes from your church. Perhaps you have a professional writer who can take this on. Go for quality – this could not only be a resource for door-to-door, but also for your open air outreach.

2 **Welcome Newcomers.** When new people move into your area pay them a welcome visit. Ask if you can help them. Give them an information pack on the best schools and restaurants in that area, and on your church.

3 **Street Parties.** Encourage people in your church to have a barbecue, or organise a street party, and invite their neighbours. You could include a light programme of drama and songs from church members.

4 **Special Services – Christmas, Easter, Harvest.** Have a Christmas Carol service each year and invite the people you have contacted in

continued over

the past 12 months. During the service present the gospel message in an attractive but penetrating way. You could use specially prepared invitations.

5 **Produce a Cassette for Distribution around Your Area.** This could include testimonies and music together with an explanation of who you are and when and where you meet. A contact phone number for enquiries or requests for practical help or prayer is essential.

6 **Follow-up.** Plan a strategy as to how you are going to follow-up on the contacts you have made. It is important that the same people visit again unless it is inappropriate. Keep a record of the key contacts so that you can inform them of events.

7 **Street Discussion Group.** You could set up a discussion group for those people in a particular street or group of streets who have shown an interest in Christianity, or are in need of friendship.

8 **Questionnaire.** This is a good way to get people talking as it is less threatening. Devise a questionnaire that will enable you to find out the social and spiritual climate of the area. This will help guide you in your prayers and will provide a base for future door-to-door work. These could also be used to stimulate conversations.

C. Action Plan!

THE 'EVERY HOME FOR CHRIST' STRATEGY

Every Home for Christ has developed a strategy to deliver evangelistic literature throughout the world personally. March for Jesus is supporting this project in the United Kingdom and recommends it as a way of delivering high-quality material and systematically making personal contact with every home in your neighbourhood.

WHY LITERATURE?

Using literature has distinct strengths:

- ☞ It never compromises its message, loses its temper, and is never intimidated.
- ☞ It doesn't get tired, or discouraged or sick.
- ☞ It always catches the person at the right time – because it only speaks as the reader chooses to read.
- ☞ It is more permanent than the human voice because it continues to speak long after the spoken words are forgotten.

WHAT IS THE EVERY HOME FOR CHRIST APPROACH?

With the Every Home for Christ strategy a personal approach is taken. In this way it is different from most leafleting today. The literature is addressed personally, and handed over with a smile, some friendly words, and prayer. The envelope contains two pieces of full-colour evangelistic literature – one for adults and one for children. It also has a reply card through which someone can:

- ☞ Ask for information.
- ☞ Request a visit.
- ☞ Indicate their desire to accept Jesus Christ as their Saviour.

No one in your church need be left out from your Every Home for Christ outreach. One team can address and stuff envelopes, another can pray, another make the visits, and yet another take responsibility for follow-up.

With an Every Home for Christ outreach, you will:

- ☞ Systematically visit every home in your community and personally deliver a printed gospel message.
- ☞ Identify and meet the needs of those who respond, and provide a contact with the local church.
- ☞ Involve the entire church by encouraging each member to use their spiritual gifts.

Teams of two go to every home – from high-rise to detached 'with a pool'. With this strategy you join hands with millions of believers, world-wide, who are taking the gospel to every home within their own communities. You also play your part to reach the whole of the UK.

Any church of 50 adult members could comfortably manage to sow the gospel into 1000 homes in their neighbourhood.

The value of an Every Home for Christ visitation programme is that:

- ☞ It is flexible – suitable for just one church – or a whole group of local churches.
- ☞ It stimulates prayer.
- ☞ It can involve everyone whatever their gifts.
- ☞ It can complement a programme

of evangelistic events.

☞ It makes a statement to your community.

☞ It will stimulate church growth.

GETTING STARTED

There is a free information pack, that provides:

☞ Samples of the literature.

☞ A detailed description of what is involved, including how to plan, how to involve others, and how to use the electoral roll to address envelopes.

☞ Details of a twelve-minute video, 'Opportunity Knocks', available for £5.95. This shares the vision and gives guidance to those who will be delivering the literature.

☞ An order form for materials.

Every Home for Christ requires that participating churches must:

☞ Make a commitment to a basic prayer programme.

☞ Keep accurate records of which homes they visit and provide this information to the Every Home for Christ national register.

☞ Plan a follow-up programme.

USE THE FORM ON PAGE 92 TO OBTAIN THE EVERY HOME FOR CHRIST INFORMATION PACK.

D. Resources

EVERY HOME FOR CHRIST,
71 Clifton Road, Shefford,
Bedfordshire SG17 5AG. 0462
815389.

THERE IS HOPE,
12 Montpelier Park, Edinburgh,
Scotland EH10 4NJ. 031 229 0003.

Stream 7 The Street Dynamic

A. INTRODUCTION

The average Briton is gripped by an instinctive horror at the thought of thrusting their beliefs on unsuspecting shoppers. Images of the hard-eyed Bible thumper haunt them.

Yet street evangelism can be entertaining and fun, a pleasure to watch rather than a source of embarrassment, and an opportunity to build relationships. Taking the gospel to the streets can be the only way for some people to have contact with Christianity or Church at all. It gives the options of listening, criticising, choosing or deciding to find out more. It sows seed about the gospel, and raises the profile of your church in the community.

We can take our cue from Jesus who went to the people in the market place and they loved it. This continued when Peter took to the street, preaching on the day of Pentecost and 3000 were saved in one go.

If God did things like this with the early Church, then there is no reason why He shouldn't do the same, and greater, with us in our streets and precincts.

So arm yourself with a love for God and people that helps overcome fear, plan creatively so that what you do opens people to your message, and take Jesus to your streets.

B. Ideas File

1 **Conversation.** Simply talk with people and build friendships. It is best to work in pairs – male and female. Apart from a simple "Excuse me, could we talk with you about Jesus?", there are a range of conversation starters. Be relaxed and be prepared to listen. Don't take it personally if some don't want to talk, there will be many who will.

Surveys about beliefs or with a gospel theme open up non-threatening opportunities to talk about the Lord. Community surveys will provide prayer and action points. Offering literature helps make contact and can explain who you are, publicise coming events or be a more direct gospel message.

2 **Preaching.** Proclamation of the truth is powerful. It should be short, carefully prepared and to the point. Avoid religious jargon and relate religious truths to the everyday life of your listener. He or she needs to understand how Christ will redirect their lives and help them face their immediate problems. Be creative. Limit it to a maximum of five minutes.

3 **Praise and Worship.** Use good musicians and a group of no less than 20 people. People with smiling, happy faces, singing and excited, will draw a crowd. Choose songs with lots of energy and make sure they are sung that way. An occasional hymn attracts the attention of older listeners.

4 **Attention-Getters.** Be creative about attracting attention to your open air. Use whacky costumes, one man bands, a performing monkey who is your best mate dressed up! Use seasonal cues like Easter and Christmas. Draw the crowd into these if you can. Ideas like the 'Strong Man' – a member of your group who has mastered ripping telephone directories in half, or the 'Flying Man' – someone in a silly costume who will jump off a step ladder to be caught by a human net of group members – can work well. Abstract backdrops work well too. Get a couple of the team sitting on stools in their camping gear for about five minutes – that will soon pull a crowd!

5 **Drama.** There are many books advising about simple, workable street drama but why not try writing your own – it often works best. Try these pointers:
- Simplicity – get across one simple idea at a time.
- Be very visual.
- Use humour – it opens people's hearts.
- Be loud – attract attention.
- Use crowd responses and draw in people in the crowd if it looks like they'll play along.
- Think about length: For shock tactics, a loud, wild 30 second whacky crowdpuller is good. To communicate a message once you have your crowd, two to five minutes should be the maximum – unless you are exceptional you are unlikely to hold people for

continued over

longer. Something like a pantomime on the streets can be longer as the crowd knows the story and, therefore, how long they will have to stay watching.

6 **Dance.** Good dance can make a joyful impact and will draw a crowd. A 'ghetto-blaster' could provide music.

7 **Visual Impact.** Street artists usually draw a crowd. The Open Air Campaigners technique of using a sketch-board is also effective. Alternatively, use mounted pictures prepared beforehand to illustrate your talk. The latest newspaper or magazine cuttings can also work well.

Jesus used everyday things such as bread or treasure to apply spiritual truths. We can do the same. Draw on posters and signs on display near your open air meeting as talking points. A well-crafted banner with a Christian message could be a visual magnet to your open air meeting. Don't use scruffy felt-tip placards! Busking is also good.

8 **Testimonies.** Testimonies should be about two minutes long. Introduce yourself by name and what you do. Go on to say how God has personally affected your life without going back to the year dot. Practise your testimonies.

Remember, no Christian jargon, or the person on the street will not understand. Don't use terms like 'saved', 'born again', 'redeemed'. They are meaningful to us, but not to others.

9 **Literature.** If you are holding regular open air meetings, consider having your own literature printed. Introduce your church and some of the members as well as giving the times of your services and activities. Make it attractive. A small, grubby tract is likely to end up on the pavement! A free literature table in the right location offers opportunities to talk. This works well in connection with any other type of street work or as an alternative form of outreach.

10 **Praise Marches and Pageants.** These make an impact both in the community and in the spiritual realm! Travelling through the streets on decorated trucks or floats, waving colourful banners and wearing fancy dress, attracts attention by creating a fun atmosphere whilst communicating the gospel through prayer and worship.

11 **Gifts.** People like to receive gifts! Lots of things can be given out on the streets – mince pies, coffee, cakes, cards, pizza. It is a good

illustration of receiving a gift freely and an opening to explain the gospel! This works well in connection with open airs.

12 **Pray for People.** This shows that both you and God care and will give you a spiritual in-road. People will rarely say "no" if you are not 'religious' about it.

C. Action Plan!

1: THE OPEN AIR

Open air meetings are a worthwhile component of any continuing programme of public outreach. The second Action Plan explains how you could integrate them into such a programme. Open airs need to be fast-moving, able to grab attention from passers-by and communicate something of God's love and what it is like to be a Christian – even when someone only pauses for a moment.

This requires creative planning because people are bombarded with so many messages. But don't be discouraged, the simplest ideas can be the most effective. Be ready for some rejection and setbacks but hold on to your goal of introducing people to Jesus. Remember that you are working with God and you are not out there alone.

PROGRAMME

Plan a varied programme of different modules. You will find plenty of concepts in the Ideas File. Use a confident master of ceremonies to hold the different elements together so that the crowd stays on through the changes.

Have the elements follow on as quickly as possible. Brief the whole group about the programme so they know when they are 'on'.

Have someone allocated to deal with any problems which may arise from drunks, worried policemen or aggressive hecklers.

Suggested programme

Praise and Worship	4mins
Introduction	3mins
Drama	5mins
Testimony	3mins
Dance	4mins
Worship	3mins
Preaching	5mins
Worship	3mins

BUILDING LINKS

Have team members mingle in the crowd to chat with those who stop and watch. When a main presentation finishes, move quickly to engage them in conversation. Our aim should be that no-one stops and listens without being spoken to. Don't get into conversation while people are watching the main presentation. Notice them during this time and pray for them. You only have two seconds to get into conversations: be quick! Ask open-ended questions like, "What did you think of that?" "What did you think of the God stuff?" If you feel it is appropriate, challenge them, "Is there any reason why you shouldn't become a Christian now?" – They can only say "no"!

Give room for the supernatural. Be listening to God for what He's saying to that person. Try to pray for the person – people are surprisingly open to being prayed for.

FORMATION

With a big group form a tight semi-circle with the leader somewhere in the middle with the musicians. The open side of the semi-circle should obviously point towards the crowd. This gives you something of a natural theatre for your dramas. Some can also form your own audience. Nothing draws a crowd like a crowd! You may also want to position people around the area distributing literature and striking up conversations. This is an important job so use people who are good communicators. The number of conversations will normally increase as the open air continues. People need to be adaptable and ready to take opportunities.

SITE AND PA

Choose a site like a shopping plaza, park or bandstand where people loiter. Permission from the owners may be needed but the general rule seems to be "don't cause any obstruction and don't litter."

Under English Common Law you are guaranteed freedom of speech and assembly in a public place. Do not cause an obstruction or disturb the peace. By-laws may mean you need special permissions. Check this with local authorities. It is a wise courtesy to inform the local police of your plans.

In many places the use of PA systems is against local by-laws, but discreet use at low levels is normally acceptable. Avoid over-loud music or preaching. People feel annoyed if you intrude on them.

C. Action Plan!

2: FOUR-WEEK PROGRAMME

This four-week programme of street evangelism builds different strategies together so that you increase the impact of your outreach. Why not choose the month leading up to a March for Jesus event to give you focus for this?

1 FIRST WEEK

Railway Stations – 1 morning, 1 evening
Send a group to go to a local railway station for the morning and evening rush hour. A longer leaflet or tract works well for mornings, as the train journey gives time to read.

Prayerwalk – 1 evening
Meet together to pray, then prayerwalk in pairs around your area. Meet again afterwards for refreshments and to compare notes.

Worship on the Streets – 1 evening
This is designed to build our sense of the presence of God in the area, rather than to communicate with people who may be around.

Take small groups to places which people felt were significant when they prayerwalked earlier in the week. Worship and pray at these places.

Open Air – Saturday morning
Meet at 10 a.m. for about an hour of prayer, worship and orientation. Then proceed with the open air.

2 SECOND WEEK

Literature Table – 1 morning, 1 afternoon
Two or more people to take a table to a busy area. A variety of tracts, leaflets, gospels and booklets can be given away. Providing free coffee could help start conversations. Have a sign explaining who you are.

Street Questionnaires – 1 morning, 1 afternoon
Firstly meet to pray, go out in pairs using questionnaires and meet again afterwards to compare notes.

Open Air – Saturday morning
As previous week.

3 THIRD WEEK

Coffee at Bus Stops – 2 mornings
This is aimed at early morning bus

queues. Set up a small table at a bus stop and provide free coffee and tea. Give away literature and get into conversations. The bus drivers may want a coffee too!

Youth Evangelism – 1 evening

Set out in pairs to places where youth are known to 'hang out'. Chat with them – have a few booklets, tracts or gospels available. Having a pizza party or some other kind of event to invite them back to is ideal.

Open Air – Saturday morning

As previous weeks.

4 FOURTH WEEK

Street Evangelism in Pairs – 1 morning, 1 afternoon

Meet for prayer first, then go out in pairs with leaflets and tracts to busy shopping areas or parks. Meet afterwards to share response.

Open Air – Friday evening

Meet about 8 p.m. for prayer and orientation then go out. This depends on having suitable areas for open airs. Shopping precincts with restaurants, pubs and cinemas are good. Some town squares and housing estates would also work.

Prayer/Praise March – Saturday morning

D. Resources

How To Present Jesus In The Open Air
Mike Sprenger (Word Publishers)
Spirits Of The City
Floyd McClung (Kingsway)
Streetwise
John Goodfellow and Andy Butcher (Kingsway)
Taking Our Cities For God
John Dawson (Word Publishers)

Christian Growth Tapes On Streetwork
by Phil Collins available from: Youth Alive Ministries, PO Box 7, Bedworth, NUNEATON, Warks CV12 9NW. 0203 643415.
Open Air Campaigners,
102 Dukes Ave., Muswell Hill, London N10 2QA. 081 444 5254
Open Air Campaigners (Australia)
PO Box 1073, Bankstown, 2200 NS Wales, Australia. 0270 96325.

Practical
Tools

PRACTICAL TOOL A
Event Check-List

The following areas are those most likely to be needed for organising an event. Remember to ask the questions:

- ☞ Who?
- ☞ What?
- ☞ When?
- ☞ Where?
- ☞ How?

Set up teams of helpers if possible so that the workload can be shared. It is advisable to confirm arrangements in writing and send a brief to key people.

Venue
Access
Locking-up time
Contact

Publicity
Press, Photography, Posters/Handbills/Tickets, Advertisements

Budget

Performers/Speakers

Chairs

Decoration

Lighting

PA

Security/Clearing Team

Counselling

Ticket Collectors

Errand Runner

PRACTICAL TOOL B
Organising a Guest Meeting

The speaker was certainly in fine form. His points were clear, his illustrations enlightening, his humour engaging. There was no doubt this was an excellent gospel presentation. There was only one problem – there were no guests to hear it.

Years ago, the Sunday evening 'Gospel Service' was considered by many to be an essential ingredient of local church life. It didn't matter that the preaching was to the converted.

Thankfully, there are many churches these days that are realising that strategic evangelistic meetings need careful thought, prayer, preparation and planning – and they don't have to happen every week!

Here are a few things to consider in planning successful guest meetings:

GUEST MEETINGS NOT 'SERVICES'

In Acts you won't find one service – but lots of meetings. People came together to bless God and one another. So be creative in planning outreach events. Sometimes the guest event WILL contain worship and preaching – or it might be a meal, a cabaret or a family picnic.

CLEAR OBJECTIVES

Is this event 'sowing' or 'reaping'? Be sure to ask the church, perhaps through housegroups, what kind of events they feel will be helpful.

TIMING

Consider carefully whether the timing suits your 'target' group.

PROVIDE PLENTY OF NOTICE

Most people live busy lives so give invitations well in advance. Some churches use well-printed invitation cards with an RSVP. Advertising is an option.

WELCOME

A friendly welcome is very important. Make sure church members are there early enough to welcome visitors. It shouldn't be left to a small appointed group. Nor is it enough for the person who is hosting the event to offer a general welcome, though that should happen as well. Make your guests feel at home and relaxed. If you have brought friends, sit with them, and be ready to explain what is happening – quietly!

Guest meetings also serve to introduce people to church life. If the event has a fixed programme, make sure there is opportunity for people to chat. It's good to have some publicity about the church and future events available. The jump between a guest meeting and the regular life of the church can be a big leap for some. Encourage people to invite guests for a meal or coffee after the event.

CONTENT

Don't be boring! It is a scandal that so often this amazing God that we serve has been projected as a cosmic bore by the Church. The programme should be well thought through, creative and multi-dimensional. Why not use drama, dance, song, poetry, coherent testimony and mime? It's especially good if you can use local people, because they can be a special pull. Of course some honest quality control will be required.

LENGTH

The event should not be too long and should start on time! Preaching should be brief and include both personal experience and Biblical content. Why not use the experiences of others? Pause briefly three or four times to let these people speak. Let any testimony or presentation be honest – not an unreal 'bed-of-roses' type picture of the Christian life.

REALITY IN WORSHIP

Guest events should reflect your church life. If worship is part of the evening, then worship as you normally would, without fear or inhibition. Some explanations may be needed to limit confusion among your guests.

COUNSELLING

Make sure there are competent people to counsel those wanting to make a commitment to Christ. Have good literature on hand and provide a warm, quiet place to chat and pray. Make sure that your counsellors are ready and alert to pick up on people who have responded.

PRACTICAL TOOL C
The Samaritan Strategy Study Notes

This set of seven studies is designed to help your church grasp from the Bible WHY you should be reaching out to those in need.

❶ A GOOD NEIGHBOUR

1 Pray, asking God to bring understanding of the passage and vision, for what it could mean for you individually and as a church.

2 Ask three people to read Luke 10:25-37, each taking a different part, i.e. narrator, law expert, Jesus.

3 Briefly discuss the needs of the injured man. How urgent was his situation?

4 As a group, imagine yourselves as the priest, the Levite and then the Samaritan. What excuses and reasons are there for your actions?

5 Jesus told this story to illustrate what neighbourly love is all about. Share what you think it means. Who is your 'neighbour' in the 90s?

6 Share why "loving your neighbour as yourself" sometimes doesn't happen. Explore practical ways in which this could be turned around.

7 Divide the group into threes to discuss concerns and ideas about showing neighbourly love – particular people with needs, fears, lack of real contact with people, creative ideas for action.

8 Pray for each other. Plan to ask each other next time how things have gone since studying and praying together.

❷ LISTENERS FIRST

1 Pray, asking God to help you listen to each other and to the Holy Spirit.

2 Ask the group to share 'feeling' words to describe what it's like not to be listened to, and to be listened to. Write them up in two separate columns on a large piece of paper.

3 Get different group members to read James 1:19; Proverbs 18:13,

25:20, 10:19. Summarise together what these verses are saying about the need to listen to people. Discuss how you can tell when someone is not listening to you. Why do you think it's important to be good listeners?

4   Divide into threes. One person share a recent incident in their lives, another person listen and help them share by asking questions, while the third person should say nothing and observe what is going on. Take no longer than five minutes.

5   Bring the group back together again. Ask the talkers, listeners and observers to tell the group how they found the experience. Is there anything here you can learn about how to be good listeners?

6   Ask someone to read Luke 10:38-42. What does this passage teach you about listening?

7   Look again at the sheet of paper with the 'feeling' words on it. Refer back to the last study where you explored what it meant to be good neighbours. Spend a few minutes in silence reflecting on these. What is the Holy Spirit saying to you about listening and future action?

8   Pray together about what you have learnt and for a deepening desire to listen to Jesus and so be more effective for Him in the world.

❸ CARING AND THE FAMILY

1   In this study you will be looking at Christians' responsibility to love their families. Be sensitive as some group members may no longer have close family. Encourage the group to see the Biblical understanding of family is much broader than that held by modern Western society.

2   Ask two people to pray. Take time to thank God for being your heavenly Father.

3   Play a word association game by writing the word 'family' on a sheet of paper and asking the group to say whatever words come into their minds as they see it. Don't let people think for too long – be fast-moving.

4   Explore how group members see family life in Britain in the 90s – strengths, weaknesses, pressures and potential.

5   Read Isaiah 58:6-7. This is God speaking to His people about the outworking of true relationship with Him. List the actions described in these verses. Where does family responsibility fit in?

6   Ask two people to read Matthew 15:1-6 and John 19:25-27. Get the group to imagine that they were onlookers of both these conversations

and to describe what they would have thought and felt. Then discuss Jesus' attitude to family responsibility.

7   Give each group member a piece of paper and pen – people should not share what they write unless they want to. List family members and other significant people in your life. Then draw a picture with yourself at the centre and the other people situated as close or far away as you feel them to be. In the gap on the paper between you and the others write the reasons for the gap.

8   Next, still alone, reflect on the needs of each of those 'family' members. How could you be involved in helping with those needs? Is there practical action to be taken that will narrow the gap?

9   Share and pray together in twos. You could pray for each other concerning the things you've written down, or if that's too personal, then in more general terms about the people you've listed.

NOTE: **This study may have stirred up issues in people's lives that will need pastoral and prayerful follow-up. Please be sensitive to this possibility.**

❹ CARING IN THE CHURCH

1   Start with group members praying one-sentence prayers thanking God for specific ways in which He has shown His care.

2   Use a large sheet of paper to write up a group description of the 'ideal caring church'. What attitudes and types of action would characterise it? Add Bible verses if you know them.

NOTE: **It would be helpful if you have done preparation on this beforehand, but don't have so many verses that group members feel undermined!**

3   Read the description of the Jerusalem church in Acts 4:32-35. Explore together what attitudes you think were held by the believers in order to make this situation possible.

4   Discuss what hinders you reaching out in care to each other as Christians. Are there particular types of people or situations that you are more reluctant to get involved with?

5   Consider practical ways in which you could overcome those barriers to lead you to caring action. How could you help each other in this?

6   Discuss how aware you think you are as a church of each other's needs.

How could this awareness be helped to grow? Brainstorm together some real possibilities.

7 Divide into fours. Refer back to Acts 4:32-35. While it may not be necessary to duplicate entirely their way of life, how can your church show similar attitudes? Come up with some creative and practical ideas. Avoid negativity and criticism!

8 Share the thinking of the small groups with the whole group. Then close by saying the 'grace' to each other, praying for each other and your church as a whole.

❺ CARING IN SOCIETY

1 Begin by dividing into twos and sharing how you became Christians. In particular, what place did the love of Christians have in the process of your coming to Christ?

2 Pray briefly in your twos, thanking God for His love demonstrated in salvation. Pray also that as a result of this study you might all gain something more of God's 'heart' for people, especially those who are vulnerable.

3 Read Isaiah 58:6-14. What types of need amongst people is God described as being passionately concerned about? List the needs on paper in one column and then the action outlined in these verses in another column.

4 Now have the group imagine they are describing British society, its needs and attitudes, to a foreign visitor. What would you say?

5 Compare that description with the lists from Isaiah 58. What similarities are there?

6 What implications does this passage have for individual Christians and the local church for involvement in caring action in society?

7 There may be a 'reality gap' between what you've read in Isaiah 58 and what you and your church are currently doing. Divide into threes and share practical ideas about how to begin to bridge that gap! How can people in your church be helped to gain a greater vision for this? You could tackle this generally or focus on one or two of the listed needs.

8 Bring the group back together to pool ideas. Is there further information, resources and expertise needed in order for you to move into caring action? Remember that the next two studies will be concentrating on your involvement in your local community.

9   Pray at the end. Thank God for His love. Pray that you and your church would see an increasing overflow of that love towards others.

❻ CARING IN YOUR COMMUNITY

1   Bring a street map of the locality with you that can be written on. Start the study in silence. Close your eyes and visualise yourself stepping out of your front door. In your imagination walk slowly away from your home and through your community. Then pray out loud, briefly, for that community.

Or you could meet as a group at the church at an earlier time than normal.

Go for a slow walk around the locality – approx. 40 minutes – praying as you go for the people in the houses as you pass. Pray that love, goodness and the peace of God would be released into that community. Pray also that God would help you see it as He sees it, and give you His heart for the people there.

2   Share together your perceptions of your community. Use descriptive words to illustrate the good and negative aspects of community life.

3   What are the main problems and needs? How do you know that these are there? Consider whether there are any other ways to gain more understanding of the community.

4   Look together at the street map. Mark on it the places where local people would go for help and for social contact. These would include Samaritans, medical centres, pubs, statutory helping agencies, library.

5   Have you marked any churches on the map? Was yours among them? Discuss together whether you think local people see your church as somewhere to come for help. Don't forget to give some reasons for your answers!

6   Read Luke 4:14-21. Using this passage, put into your own words what Jesus came to do. Explore together how far you think He calls us to do these things too.

7   Now read Matthew 25:31-46. In threes discuss the attitudes that lie behind the action and the possible practical local application by you/your church of the care described here.

8   Share your thinking with the group. See if any common strands or ideas emerge. Note them down for future reference.

9   Spend the rest of the time in prayer, keeping the map as a visual aid

and recalling the thoughts that you've had about your local community and its needs.

10 Is there any action, apart from a community survey, that you need to take in order to understand more fully the 'heartbeat' of your locality? It could include asking the opinion of key local people concerning the needs of the community, e.g. pub landlords, shop-keepers, community beat police officers or finding out what services and caring initiatives there are already available in the locality.

❼ INTO THE COMMUNITY

The purpose of this meeting is to prepare for carrying out a community survey. Make available to every group member a copy of the community survey and notes for interviewers – see next section.

1 Look through the notes together. Make sure that you are clear about why you are doing the survey. Discuss who you are aiming at and how you are going to do it.

2 Decide on your catchment area, picking a good cross-section of the community. Divide up the streets and homes amongst those who will be carrying out the survey.

3 Now go through the questions. Do they need adapting in order to find the information you want? Or to suit your particular community, e.g. if there is a particular ethnic mix of people?

4 Discuss and decide together how the information from the questionnaires will be collated, acted upon immediately where necessary, and shared with the church and community in appropriate ways at a later stage.

5 Read John 20:21-22. Apply what these verses say to yourselves as you move into more active involvement in the community.

6 Spend the rest of the time in prayer – both for what happens on the survey and for the follow-up of it.

DON'T FORGET!

☛ To make sure that you have agreed with the church leaders what you plan to do.

☛ Have a team of volunteers ready to give practical assistance and prayer support during the survey week.

☛ Don't start something that you can't follow through in people's lives in your community.

PRACTICAL TOOL D
Community Survey Questionnaire

NOTES FOR INTERVIEWERS

You may want to adapt this questionnaire for your local community or to identify more specific areas of need.

AIMS

☛ To gain a deeper understanding of the nature of the local community – strengths, weaknesses, neighbourliness, social centres, etc.

☛ To gain a clearer understanding of individual and community 'felt' needs rather than relying on assumptions.

☛ To raise the general profile of your church and more specifically as a caring group of people who want their Christianity to be relevant and practical in its expression.

☛ To prepare the way for a new project by raising people's awareness. It is not a questionnaire that is geared towards creating opportunities for personal evangelism, but questions 14 and 16 will lend themselves to this if so desired.

USE

The questionnaire is best completed by means of personal interview rather than distributed through the post. You should introduce yourself by name and by church, politely requesting a few minutes of the respondent's time to help you with the survey. Explain that your church is concerned to find out what people think about the area and its needs, including their own personal needs. This is so that you can be actively involved as a church in serving the community and being a part of it in a way that makes a positive contribution.

FOLLOW UP

If at all possible, it is important to follow up the questionnaire by making the results available to the community. This can be done in several ways: distributing a circular letter around the neighbourhood, submitting the findings in the form of an article to the local newspaper and/or free press, or putting a poster up outside the church.

When you advertise the actual project you can refer back to the questionnaire. In so doing, you communicate the fact that you are prepared to listen to people and take what they think seriously.

COMMUNITY SURVEY

1 Age
Under 21 ☐   21-45 ☐   46-65 ☐   Over 65 ☐

2 Sex
Male ☐ Female ☐

3 Occupation

_____   Unemployed ☐

4 Do you/your partner work locally?
Within 1 mile ☐   2-5 miles ☐   Further ☐

5 How long have you lived in this area?
Under 1 year ☐   1-5 years ☐   6-10 years ☐   Longer ☐

6 How many people do you talk to in a day from outside the home?

(Face-to-face) _____

7 Would you and your neighbours visit one another?
Several times a week ☐   Occasionally ☐   Rarely ☐   Never ☐

8 What sort of neighbourhood is this generally?
Friendly ☐ Unfriendly ☐

9 What do you see as the main problems in the area?

_____

_____

_____

10 What facilities do you think are lacking in this area?
(a) Generally, e.g. leisure, help with difficulties, etc.

_____

(b) For different age groups, e.g. elderly, young people, unemployed, women, etc.

_____

11 Who would you look to for help in a time of crisis? *(Can tick more than one)*

Cope on your own if at all possible ☐   Doctor ☐   Church ☐
A neighbour ☐   Family member ☐   Friend ☐   Other ☐ (specify)

12 Where would you recommend someone to go locally if they want to

(a) Meet new people

(b) Have a good time

(c) Have advice about a personal problem

13 If you have any questions about things like life after death, the meaning of your life, etc. to whom would you talk? *(Can tick more than one)*

Family ☐   Friend ☐   Someone that is 'religious' ☐   Other ☐

(specify)

14 Do you attend church?

Regularly ☐   Rarely ☐   Never ☐

CALLED TO ACTION

15 What would you like to see the church do in this area?

16 What do you think of the church today generally?

Thank you very much for your help in completing this questionnaire. This community survey has been reproduced with the kind permission of Fount Publishers.

PRACTICAL TOOL E
Just Looking Groups

Not many people become Christians the first time they hear the gospel. Some do, of course. God's grace can't be limited. But most need time to think through the message, sort it out in their minds, and make their decision thoughtfully.

That's why 'Just Looking' type groups have become an important method of evangelism. Just Looking was invented as a means of following up school missions to teenagers. Instead of challenging young people to become Christians on the spot – which often resulted in premature responses which didn't last – they were challenged to join a small group in which they would investigate Christianity thoroughly for five weeks. During the five weeks, they would be guaranteed three conditions – "no pressure", "no boredom" and "no embarrassment" – and there would be no strings attached. They would be able to walk away at the end without having been made to feel that they were failures.

Under these conditions, many were attracted. Instead of five or six long-lasting decisions from each school mission, we started to see an average of seventy-five teenagers sign-up for Just Looking groups. And over the five weeks, three-quarters of them would find their way to faith.

Several different systems have now been pioneered and Just Looking itself has been widely used among adults as well as teenagers. It's built on several key principles:

1   The ideal size of the group is around six (one Christian, five enquirers). One other Christian can be involved so as to "learn on the job", but non-Christians must be in a clear majority!

2   The meetings last for one hour exactly. If people want to stay afterwards, that's fine, but it must be possible for participants to leave after sixty minutes without embarrassment.

3   The course is based around simple Bible study, each week answering a key question which non-Christians ask, gradually building up a picture of what the gospel actually is.

4   The course contains three elements: *explanation* of the content of the gospel; *evidence* for the truth of it (extra hand-out sheets and further reading suggestions are available every week); and *experience* – personal testimony is important, and on two of the five weeks a Christian who is a "good advert" for the faith is invited along to share his or her

story and answer questions.

5 An introduction to the gospel should also be an introduction to God's family, so there is one trip to church included in the course – for the whole group together between weeks four and five. The church is advised that they are coming and a leader from the church comes to the group in its final week to answer questions about the way the service was conducted. Everything is done to make the outsiders receive as warm and intelligible an introduction to the community of faith as we can possibly arrange.

6 Extra resources are provided outside the group meetings for those who have more questions than others. Literature and hand-outs, personal chats with the group leader and extra personal 'projects' can be requested.

7 Because people respond to Christ at a different rate, the whole course supplies as many opportunities as possible for people to indicate that they want to receive Christ. They may tick a reaction sheet each week, hand in a reply card, meet with a leader, or take one of the several other embarrassment-free opportunities to signal their decision.

8 Hymns, prayers and other religious exercises are *out*. There should be a great deal of prayer surrounding the group – but before they arrive, not during the meetings! The aim is to create an environment which will unsettle non-Christians as little as possible. The more discomfort they feel, the less they will take in what is being said – or open up themselves in discussion.

9 For that reason, it is best to form groups out of people who naturally relate well together. The fewer social hurdles they have to cross, the better the group will function.

10 If people become Christians before the group is finished (which often happens), it is best to keep them in there until the end. You can always meet with them separately for prayer and Bible study. Often one new Christian in a group will act as a catalyst. As others witness what has happened, it prompts them to make the big jump too!

11 At the end, the leader should try to stay in touch with the group members, even where no response has been made. They should feel that your friendship isn't conditional upon their accepting your message! And often it is in the weeks following a Just Looking group, when former members start to miss it and remember some of the things they were learning, that it all clicks into place and a decision can be made.

D. Resources

Just Looking
John Allan (Bible Society)

Christian Basics
(Church Pastoral Aid Society)
An ambitious video-based course
allowing a church to tackle four
areas of ministry including Just
Looking type groups and nuture
groups for new Christians,
utilising the same set of resources.
Expensive but thorough.

Good News Down Your Street
Michael Wooderson
A simple approach (from which
the original Just Looking pinched
a lot of ideas!) by which a church
can send three members to run a
group in someone's own home for
six weeks. Enormously effective,
with regular training courses run
by The Network Trust, 100 Lazy
Hill Road, Aldridge, Walsall WS9
8RR.

PRACTICAL TOOL F
Additional Resources

Some of these books may be out of print but if you can get hold of them you
will find them extremely useful.

Effective Evangelism
Floyd McClung (Marshall Pickering)

An Evangelism Cookbook
Derek Cook (Paternoster Press)

Evangelism Explosion
D James Kennedy (Evangelism
Explosion Ltd)

Evangelism Now And Then
Michael Green (IVP)

**Evangelism Through The Local
Church**
Michael Green (Hodder &
Stoughton)

A Guide To Evangelism
Clive Calver, Derek Copley, Bob
Moffett and Jim Smith ed. (Marshall
Pickering)

How To Give Away Your Faith
Paul Little (IVP)

**Know And Tell The Gospel: Help
For The Reluctant Evangelist**
John Chapman (Hodder and
Stoughton)

Mission Possible
Malcolm Egner (SU)

Power Evangelism
John Wimber (Hodder and
Stoughton)

The Reluctant Evangelist
Paul Miller (Kingsway)

Sharing Your Faith
Selwyn Hughes (Marshall Pickering)

EVANGELICAL ALLIANCE
Whitefield House, 186 Kennington
Park Road, London SE11 4BT.
071 582 0228.

ICHTHUS
107-113 Stanstead Road, Forest Hill,

London SE23 1HH. 081 291 4057.

MARCH FOR JESUS
PO Box 39, Sunbury-On-Thames,
Middlesex TW16 6PP. 0932 789681.

PIONEER
PO Box 79c, Esher, Surrey KT10
9LP. 0372 463051.

YOUTH WITH A MISSION
13 Highfield Oval, Ambrose Lane,
Harpenden, Herts AL5 4BX. 05827
65481.

YOUTH WITH A MISSION
PO Box 61, Watson, ACT 2602,
Australia.

YOUTH WITH A MISSION
PO Box 94187, Richmond BC, V6Y
2A3. Canada.

YOUTH WITH A MISSION
PO Box 13-580, Auckland 1132, New
Zealand.

YOUTH WITH A MISSION
305-354 Shaw Plaza, 352 Balestier
Road, Singapore 1232, Singapore.

YOUTH WITH A MISSION
Private Bag 10, Garden View 2047,
Johannesburg, South Africa.

The resources mentioned in this
Evangelism Toolkit do not form an
exhaustive list of the materials
available today. Nor are they the
only resources we would
recommend. Those included in this
manual have been chosen as
examples.

MARCH FOR JESUS

From its start in Britain in 1987, March for Jesus, a grassroots movement
uniting Christians on the streets for prayer and praise, is spreading across the
world.

Led by Roger Forster of Ichthus Christian Fellowship, Lynn Green of Youth
With A Mission, Gerald Coates of the Pioneer Team and Graham Kendrick,
March for Jesus saw 200,000 on the streets of Britain on the same day from
1989 to 1991.

The first international March for Jesus was held on 23 May 1992, uniting
over 600,000 across Europe and North America.

Whether a March for Jesus involves a cluster of local churches uniting to
celebrate Jesus in joyful procession where they live, or is a gathering of
thousands making an impact on the national capital, Christians of different
races, cultures and church backgrounds are expressing new unity as they link
across nations and continents.

The walls are being taken off the church, giving the gospel new visibility in
the community and nation. Foundations are being laid for evangelism,
churches and individual Christians are finding new boldness, and new
friendships are being built.

To March for Jesus with Christians across the world, contact the March for Jesus Office for information on dates, and resources for march organisation. **March for Jesus, PO Box 39, Sunbury on Thames, Middlesex. TW16 6PP. UK. Telephone: 0932 789681. Fax: 0932 789691.**

DOOR-TO-DOOR PLAN – EVERY HOME FOR CHRIST RESPONSE FORM

We would like to seriously investigate what would be involved in sowing the gospel to at least 1000 homes.

☐ Please send me the free Information Pack. (This includes sample full-colour leaflets, operational guide and timetable, sample record forms and an order form for materials)

☐ Please send me the 12-minute information and equipping video 'Opportunity Knocks'.

☐ Please enclose a cheque for £5.95 (payable to Every Home for Christ).

Title

Forename

Surname

Address

Postcode

Day-time Telephone

Church/Group respresented

Please send this form to Every Home for Christ, 71 Clifton Road, Shefford, Bedfordshire SG17 5AG. Tel. 0462 815389.

Further Resources for Evangelism from CWR

Details of other CWR publications produced for use in evangelism and nurture are described on the following pages.

These publications can be obtained through your local Christian bookshop or direct from CWR at the address given below.

Discounts for bulk orders are available for churches, mission organisations, etc. Please contact us for further details.

Readers overseas should contact their National Distributor. For details see page 2.

Waverley Abbey House, Waverley Lane, Farnham, Surrey GU9 8EP.
United Kingdom.
Tel. 0252 783788   Fax. 0252 783847

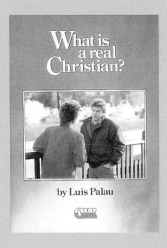

What is a Real Christian?

Luis Palau

International evangelist Luis Palau has explained what it means to be a real Christian to millions of people worldwide.

In this attractive colour booklet he examines many of the popular myths about what a Christian is. He points us clearly to the reality and shows the steps to take to become a real Christian.

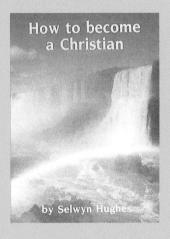

How to Become a Christian

Selwyn Hughes

An easy to understand, colourful tract. Ideal for the "man in the street".

Sold in packs of 100.

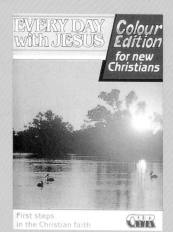

Every Day with Jesus for New Christians

Selwyn Hughes

A special edition of *Every Day with Jesus* to help new Christians with their first steps in the faith.

53 readings explore what it means to be a new person in Christ and examine stepping stones and obstacles to growing in the Christian life. Its daily reading plan will also encourage new believers in establishing a daily devotional pattern.

Every Day with Jesus for New Christians has now been read by over 1/2 million people worldwide. Illustrated in full colour. Also available in French, German, Spanish, Portuguese and Russian.

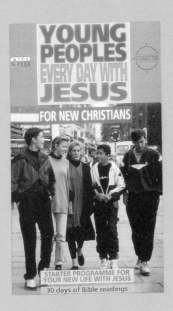

Young People's Every Day with Jesus for New Christians

Selwyn Hughes

A 30-day starter programme for teen-agers, *Young People's Every Day With Jesus for New Christians* highlights the basics of living for Jesus with a different topic and Bible reading for each day.

Practical guidelines cover the opportunities and difficulties of following God's plans for our lives, together with the resources God supplies. *Illustrated.*

Topz for New Christians

Bible readings, prayers, cartoons, puzzles, code-cracking, quizzes, colouring, jokes and much more!

Day-by-day help for 7-11 year-olds, explaining how we can become God's friends and how to grow closer to Jesus.